Billy Graham Evangelistic Association

DEAR FRIEND,

I am pleased to send you this copy of *Peace with God*.

This classic book by my father, Billy Graham, has helped thousands of people find true peace in the midst of turmoil.

If you would like to know more about the Billy Graham Evangelistic Association, please contact us toll-free at 1-877-247-2426 or via our Web site, www.billygraham.org. We would appreciate knowing how this book or our ministry has touched your life.

May God bless you.

Sincerely,

Franklin Graham
President and CEO

Therefore being justified by faith,
we have peace with God through our
Lord Jesus Christ.

Romans 5:1

PEACE with GOD

Billy Graham

This **Billy Graham Library Selection** special edition
is published with permission from W. Publishing Group
(a division of Thomas Nelson, Inc.).

W PUBLISHING GROUP™
www.wpublishinggroup.com
A Division of Thomas Nelson, Inc
www.ThomasNelson.com

PEACE WITH GOD

Unless otherwise indicated, all Scripture quotations are from the King James Version of the Bible.

Library of Congress Cataloging-in-Publication Data

Graham, Billy, 1918–
Peace with God.

1. Theology, Doctrinal—Popular works.
I. Title. BT77.G78 1984 230 84-17421
ISBN 1-59328-027-0
Previous ISBN 0-8499-0464-1
and ISBN 0-913367-43-5

A Billy Graham Library Selection designates materials that are appropriate to a well-rounded collection of quality Christian literature, including both classic and contemporary reading and reference materials.

Printed in the United States of America

A MESSAGE FROM THE BILLY GRAHAM EVANGELISTIC ASSOCIATION

If you are committing your life to Christ, please let us know! We would like to send you Bible study materials and a complimentary six-month subscription to *Decision* magazine to help you grow in your faith.

The Billy Graham Evangelistic Association exists to support the evangelistic ministry and calling of Billy Graham to take the message of Christ to all we can by every effective means available to us.

Our desire is to introduce as many as we can to the person of Jesus Christ, so that they might experience His love and forgiveness.

Your prayers are the most important way to support us in this ministry. We are grateful for the dedicated prayer support we receive. We are also grateful for those who support us with contributions.

Giving can be a rewarding experience for you and for us at the Billy Graham Evangelistic Association. Your gift gives you the satisfaction of supporting an organization that is actively involved in evangelism. Also, it is encouraging to us because part of our ministry is devoted to helping people like you discover and enjoy the stewardship of giving wisely and effectively.

Billy Graham Evangelistic Association
1 Billy Graham Parkway
Charlotte, North Carolina 28201-0001
www.billygraham.org

Toll-free (U.S.): 1-877-247-2426

Billy Graham Evangelistic Association of Canada
20 Hopewell Way NE
Calgary, Alberta T3J 5H5
www.billygraham.ca

Toll-free (Canada): 1-888-393-0003

Contents

PART THREE:
Applying the Antidote

Preface

IN THE THREE DECADES since *Peace with God* was originally written, an embattled world seems to have permanently lost its fragile grasp on serenity. For the first time in history, an entire generation of young people lives in fear that time, in the form of a nuclear holocaust, will run out before they can grow up, which may explain in part why tragic numbers of them at the peak of youthful promise find various ways to drop out of life. We have become a generation of escape artists. As I write these words, armed conflicts are raging in many places around the globe and the streets of more than one great city ring with gunfire. An American President was assassinated since the book was written, as were an Attorney General, a civil rights leader, an Egyptian President and a famous rock star. Another President was the victim of an attempted assassination. Hostages have been in many places and a Korean passenger jet shot down. Many wars have been fought. Nor can we turn to the security of our homes to find inner peace, for many of our homes simply aren't there anymore as nearly half of all new marriages now end in divorce. This strife that runs rampant in the world at large is but a reflection of the conflict storming individual hearts.

Millions have read this book in its original version. It has been translated into more than thirty languages. Thousands have written to tell how their own lives or the lives of someone else have been transformed and affected. We have been told that it is the most read and distributed religious book in the Eastern world. A customs official in one of these areas came across a copy of *Peace with God* in the luggage of a Christian visiting his country. The tourist said he would happily give it to him, but he had promised it to a friend in that country.

"Then will you wait while I read it?" the official asked. So our friend waited—half an hour, an hour, two hours. Finally, without comment, the book was returned to the suitcase and our friend was waved through. In revising it, I was amazed to find how relevant the original was, yet some details needed updating.

This revised edition, as did the original *Peace with God*, points the way, the *only* way, to authentic personal peace in a world in crisis. Since its publication thirty-one years ago, millions of readers here and in other lands have followed its clear, simple steps and discovered for themselves the revolutionary new life offered by a once unknown Galilean. These include men writing on Death Row and even one of my sons-in-law.

One of the reporters who covered our Crusade in Bristol, England, was asked if she had been involved in a church before coming to Bristol and she replied, "O yes, I'm a Christian. I was converted through Billy Graham in 1954." As a ten-year-old girl, away at boarding school, she had gone to a "jumble sale" (similar to our garage sales). On the table were a number of books. She noticed a copy of *Peace with God* and was immediately drawn to it. She paid sixpence for it—all the money she had at the moment—and stayed up all night reading it by flashlight in her room back at the school. She accepted Christ as a result of reading that book. Although she had grown up in the church, she had never had anyone explain the simple message of the gospel and how she could respond to Christ.

It is my prayer that this revised edition will find its way into the hands and hearts of a lost, confused, and searching world, for I sense that now, even more than when the book was first written, men, women, and young people everywhere thirst for peace with God.

I am deeply grateful to all those who have counseled with me in the preparation of this new edition. Special thanks are due to my wife, Ruth, who worked many hours on its revision; my oldest daughter, GiGi; and my secretary, Stephanie Wills. May God use this book to touch the lives of millions more in this new generation.

Billy Graham

Publisher's Note

SINCE its first publication over forty years ago Dr. Billy Graham's *Peace with God* has blessed us with the voice of spiritual calm through decades of war, turmoil, and world change. While some of the statistics and world situations have changed since the book's most recent revision, the need for a clear message of calmness and peace in our lives has not. Word Publishing is honored and pleased, therefore, to join Dr. Graham in reaffirming his timeless biblical message by republishing this devotional classic, as revised in 1984, so that it may continue to bring you "peace with God through our Lord Jesus Christ."

PART ONE

Assessing the Situation

1

The Great Quest

And ye shall seek me, and find me, when ye shall search for me with all your heart.

Jeremiah 29:13

YOU started on the Great Quest the moment you were born. It was many years perhaps before you realized it, before it became apparent that you were constantly searching—searching for something you never had—searching for something that was more important than anything in life. Sometimes you have tried to forget about it. Sometimes you have attempted to lose yourself in other things so there could be time and thought for nothing but the business at hand. Sometimes you may even have felt that you were freed from the need to go on seeking this nameless thing. At moments you have almost been able to dismiss the quest completely. But always you have been caught up in it again—always you have had to come back to your search.

At the loneliest moments in your life you have looked at other men and women and wondered if they too were seeking—something they couldn't describe but knew they wanted and needed. Some of them seemed to have found fulfillment in marriage and family living. Others went off to achieve fame and fortune in other parts of the world. Still others stayed at home and prospered, and looking at them you may have thought: "These people are not on the Great Quest. These people have found their way. They knew what they wanted and have been able to grasp it.

It is only I who travel this path that leads to nowhere. It is only I who goes asking, seeking, stumbling along this dark and despairing road that has no guideposts."

The Cry of Mankind

But you are not alone. All mankind is traveling with you, for all mankind is on this same quest. All humanity is seeking the answer to the confusion, the moral sickness, the spiritual emptiness that oppresses the world. All mankind is crying out for guidance, for comfort, for peace.

We are told that we live in the "age of anxiety." Historians point out that there have been few times in all history when man has been subject to so much fear and uncertainty. All the familiar props seem to have been swept away. We talk of peace but are confronted by war at every turn. We devise elaborate schemes for security but have not found it. We grasp at every passing straw and even as we clutch, it disappears.

For generations we have been running like frightened children, up first one blind alley and then another. Each time we have told ourselves: "This path is the right one, this one will take us where we want to go." But each time we have been wrong.

The Path of Political Freedom

One of the first paths we chose was labeled "political freedom." Give everyone political freedom, we said, and the world will become a happy place. Let us select our own government leaders and we shall have the kind of government that will make life worth living. So we achieved political freedom, but we did not achieve our better world. Our daily newspapers give us reports of corruption in high places, of favoritism, of exploitation, of hypocrisy equal to and sometimes surpassing the despotism of ancient kings. Political freedom is a precious and important thing, but it alone cannot give us the kind of world we long for.

There was another very hopeful path marked "education," and many put their whole faith in it. Political freedom coupled with education will do the trick, they said, and we all rushed madly along the educational path. It seemed a bright, well-lighted, sensible path for a long time, and we traveled it with eager, expectant feet, but where has it led us? You know the answer. We are the most informed people in the history of civilization—and yet the most confused. Our high school students know more about the physical laws of the universe than the greatest scientist in the days of Aristotle. But though our heads are crammed with knowledge, our hearts are empty.

The brightest, most inviting path of all was the one marked "higher standards of living." Almost everyone felt he could trust this one to carry him automatically into that better and more joyful world. This was felt to be the sure route. This was the "press the button and you're there" route! This was the path that led through the beautiful full-color magazine advertisements, past all the shining new cars, past the gleaming rows of electric refrigerators and automatic washing machines, past all the fat chickens cooking in brand-new copper-bottomed pots. We knew we'd hit the jackpot this time! The other paths might have been false leads, but this time we had it!

All right, look around you right this minute. At this very moment in history you see in America a country that has political freedom to an extent undreamed of in many parts of the civilized world. You see the greatest and most far-reaching public education system that man has ever created, and we are eulogized at home and abroad for our high standard of living. "The American way of life" we like to call this fully electrified, fully automatic, chrome-plated economy of ours—but has it made us happy? Has it brought us the joy and satisfaction and the reason for living that we were seeking?

No. As we stand here feeling smug and proud that we have accomplished so much that generations before us only dreamed about; as we span our oceans in hours instead of months; as we produce miracle drugs that wipe out some of man's most dread diseases; as we erect buildings that make the Tower of Babel seem like an anthill; as we learn more and more of the mysterious secrets that lie in the depths of the sea and probe further and further into outer space, do we lose one iota of that empty feeling within us? Do all these modern wonders bring us a sense of fulfillment, do they help to explain why we are here, do they point out what we are supposed to learn?

Or does that awful hollow feeling persist? Does every further discovery of the magnitude of the universe comfort us or make us feel more alone and helpless than ever? Does the antidote for human fear and hatred and corruption lie in some laboratory test tube, or in an astronomer's telescope?

The Seduction of Science

We cannot deny that science has given man many things he thought he wanted. But this same science has now presented us the most dreaded gift ever bestowed upon humanity. The life and future of every living being on this planet is affected by this gift of science. It stands like a somber shadow behind our waking thoughts. It stalks like a specter of horror through our children's dreams. We pretend it isn't there. We try to pretend that we haven't received this gift, that it's all a joke, and that some morning we'll wake up and find that we haven't conquered outer space and that nuclear weaponry has never been perfected—but our morning newspaper tells us a different story.

There are other paths, of course, and many are traveling them this very moment. There are the paths of fame and fortune, of pleasure and power. None of them leads anywhere but deeper into the mire. We are ensnared in the web of our own thinking, trapped so cleverly and so completely that we can no longer see either the cause or the cure of the disease that is inflicting such deadly pain.

If it is true that "for every illness there is a cure," then we must make haste to find it. The sand in civilization's hourglass is rapidly falling away, and if there is a path that leads to the light, if there is a way back to spiritual health, we must not lose an hour!

The Search for Solutions

Many are floundering in this time of crisis and finding that their efforts are leading them not up but only further down into the pit.

The suicide rate has sky-rocketed in the '80s. For children 10–14 the suicide rate has tripled in the last ten years. *Leadership* magazine estimates that half a million people attempt suicide annually—and 50,000 succeed. In 1981 more people died by suicide than by homicide.

Last year thousands of Americans, many of them teenagers, who couldn't find even the wrong answers, took their own lives in preference to wandering any further in this man-made jungle we call civilization.

Over the past couple of decades our divorce rates have soared, even within the church, with one out of two marriages ending in divorce. The divorce rate has increased 100 percent since 1900!

We spend a fortune to "adopt" cute cabbage patch dolls, while our children are caught up in child abuse or subjected to the horrible atrocities of "kiddy-porn." We hear about abortion on demand, surrogate motherhood, sperm banks, and so on. Our families are riddled with all kinds of abuses and aberrations.

So "Where are we?" you ask. "Where are we now and where are we going?" Let me tell you *where* we are and *what* we are. We are a nation of empty people. Our heads are crammed full of knowledge, but within our souls is a spiritual vacuum.

We complained in the past that the youth of this country had lost its drive, its push, its willingness to work and to get ahead. Every day I heard parents say that they didn't understand why their children didn't want to work but just wanted everything handed to them. Parents didn't seem to realize that their well-educated, carefully brought up children were actually empty inside. They weren't filled with the spirit that makes work a joy. They weren't filled with the determination that makes pushing ahead a pleasure. And why were they so empty? Because they didn't know where they had come from, why they were here, or where they were going!

Today our young people are asking for direction and perspective. They are looking for models to follow, for patterns of purpose.

They are like rows of beautiful new automobiles, perfect in every detail but with no gasoline in the tanks. The exteriors are fine, but there's nothing inside to give them power. And so they just sit and rust—with boredom.

The Breadth of Boredom

America is said to have the highest per capita boredom of any spot on earth! We know that because we have the greatest variety and greatest number of artificial amusements of any country. People have become so empty that they can't even entertain themselves. They have to pay other people to amuse them, to make them laugh, to try to make them feel warm and happy and comfortable for a few minutes, to try to lose that awful frightening, hollow feeling—that terrible, dreaded feeling of being lost and alone.

You may think that boredom is a minor matter. Everyone gets bored sometimes; it's only natural. But let me tell you something about boredom and this dangerous apathy that is creeping over the land and over the minds and hearts of the people. Man is the only one of God's creatures who is capable of being bored, although I've seen animals in a zoo that *look* very bored! No other living thing except man can ever be bored with itself or its surroundings. This is very significant, for the Creator never does anything without a purpose, and if He gave man the capacity for boredom, He did it for a purpose.

Boredom is one of the sure ways to measure your own inner emptiness! It's as accurate as a thermometer for telling just how hollow your inner spirit really is. The person who is thoroughly bored is living and working in a vacuum. His inner self is a vacuum, and there is nothing that nature resents more than a vacuum. It is one of the unfailing rules of this universe that all vacuums must be filled, and filled immediately.

A Nation of Empty People

We do not have to go back to ancient times to see what happens to a nation of empty people. We need look no further than the recent history of Germany or Italy to see with what deadly speed nature fills up the vacuums that occur within us. Nazism in Germany and fascism in Italy could find no place in the heart and soul of a person who was filled with the Spirit of God, but false ideologies flood with the greatest ease into the minds and hearts of those who are empty and waiting. Nature abhors a vacuum, but it is up to us as individuals to determine with what our inner vacuums shall be filled.

So that is where we stand today—nations of empty people. We have tried to fill ourselves with science and education, with better living and pleasure, with the many other things we thought we wanted. We have increasingly decadent capitalism at one extreme, and godless communism at the other. But we are still empty. Why are we empty? Because the Creator made us for Himself; and we shall never find completeness and fullness apart from fellowship with Him.

In a recent interview in the *Presbyterian Journal* (2 November 1983) the eminent Catholic columnist, Michael Novak, says of our situation: "Socialism is a system for saints, . . . democratic capitalism . . . is a system for sinners." That's why he feels socialism won't work in this world.

Jesus told us long ago that "Man shall not live by bread alone" (Luke 4:4), but we have paid no heed. We have tried to do just that.

We cannot stand the terrible emptiness of ourselves, we cannot look at the lonely, desolate road that lies ahead. We are desperately weary of the hatred and greed and lust that we know are within us, but we are helpless to be rid of them and be filled with something better.

"Time and tide wait for no man," said Sir Walter Scott. The tools of total annihilation have been placed within our reach. We cannot scurry up any more false paths, we cannot explore any more unknown roads, we cannot afford to be trapped in any more blind alleys. We don't have that much time! For our generation has accomplished what other generations only *tried* to do, or dreamed of doing in their most insane moments of power and ruthlessness! We have achieved the weapons of total destruction. We are witnessing the climax of man's madness—the impending nuclear holocaust.

How the demons must have laughed as some of the most brilliant men on earth worked furiously for years to achieve this horror! The atom cleaved! Divide and conquer! Split apart, destroy, shatter, crush, crumble! The great deceiver has done his work, and men have been eager to aid him. We see before us Satan's masterpiece, his clever counterfeit of the cloven tongues of divine fire. For this satanic fire and the pentecostal flames both fall from above, both are cloven, both illuminate, both instantly transform everything they touch—but with such a difference. The difference of heaven and hell!

A Topsy-turvy World

We are living in a topsy-turvy world, where all is confusion. But you may be sure that it is confusion with a plan—Satan's plan! The Bible tells us that Satan is the great deceiver and he has devoted himself to the cause of our great self-deception and to the deceptions that lie between nations all over this world. He has led us to believe that things were getting better, when they are really getting worse.

We all recognize that the world has changed radically since the beginning of this century. We are aware of its increased tempo, of the spirit of revolution that is sweeping away the established landmarks and traditions, of the speed with which language, fashions, customs, housing, and our ways of living and thinking are being altered and changed.

Only a few years ago children were delighted at the prospect of a trip to the train station to watch the trains come in. Today they are blasé about the space shuttle. How many know when the next shuttle flight takes off, or who will be aboard? We who once marveled at the telegraph now take the far greater miracle of television for granted. Not so long ago many of man's physical diseases were termed hopeless and incurable. Today, we have drugs so effective that many age-old diseases are disappearing. We have accomplished much, of that there is no doubt.

But with all this progress, man has not solved the basic

problem of the human race. We can build the highest buildings, the fastest planes, the longest bridges. We have successfully probed the far reaches of space and conquered the unknown. But we still can't govern ourselves or live together in equality and peace!

We may create great new schools of art and music, we may discover newer and better vitamins, but there is nothing new about our troubles. They are the same old ones that man has always had, only they seem magnified and more abundant. They may come upon us in new ways, they may seem to give sharper pain and deeper anguish; but fundamentally we are facing the same temptations, the same trials, the same testings that have always confronted mankind.

Forever since that tragic moment in the Garden of Eden, when man gave up God's will for his own will, man has been plagued by the same problems. Their cause is stated in the third chapter of Genesis. The terrible conditions that produced them are related in the first chapter of Romans. And the gospel of Jesus Christ gives us their remedy.

It is man's depraved and sinful nature that fills him with hate, envy, greed, and jealousy. The curse of sin is upon his body, and he is forever haunted by the fear of death. His inventive genius has enabled him to change everything but himself. For man, in spite of the loudly acclaimed "progress" of our times, remains just as he was in the beginning.

Sin Is Still the Same

Sin, too, has remained unchanged, although man has done his best to alter it. We've tried to dress it up with other names. We've put new labels on the same old bottle of poison. We've tried to whitewash the rotting building and pretend it was sound (or new).

We've tried calling sin "errors" or "mistakes" or "poor judgment," but sin itself has stayed the same. No matter how we try to salve our conscience, we've known all along that men are still sinners; and the results of sin are still disease, disappointment, disillusionment, despair, and death.

Sorrow hasn't changed, either. It began when Adam and Eve looked with broken hearts upon the lifeless body of their murdered son Abel and knew the crushing weight of grief. It has gone on, until today sorrow is the universal language of man. No one escapes it, everyone experiences it. It even seemed to one of Job's comforters that it was the aim of life, for he said, "Yet man is born unto trouble, as the sparks fly upward" (Job 5:7).

Death is also still the same. Men have tried to change its appearance. We have changed the word "undertaker" to "mortician." We place bodies in "caskets" now instead of "coffins." We have "funeral homes" instead of "undertaking parlors" and "memorial parks" instead of "graveyards." We try to soften the starkness of the last rites; but regardless of what we call it, or how lifelike we make the corpse through make-up, the cold, hard, cruel reality of death has not changed throughout all of man's history. A friend, struggling with terminal cancer, recently wrote: "It has dawned on me that cancer is not terminal—life is!"

These three facts constitute the true story of man: His past is filled with sin; his present is overflowing with sorrow; and the certainty of death faces him in the future.

The Bible says, "It is appointed unto men once to die . . ." (Hebrews 9:27), and to the average person this seems a stark and hopeless situation. Hundreds of philosophies and scores of religions have been invented by men in their efforts to circumvent the Word of God. Modern philosophers and psychologists are still trying to make it appear that there is some way out other than the path of Jesus. But man has tried them all and none of them leads anywhere but down.

Christ came to give us the answers to the three enduring problems of sin, sorrow, and death. It is Jesus Christ, and He alone, who is also enduring and unchanging, "the same yesterday, and today and forever" (Hebrews 13:8). As the hymnwriter Henry F. Lyte wrote: "Change and decay in all around I see; O Thou who changest not, abide with me."

All other things may change, but Christ remains unchangeable. In the restless sea of human passions, Christ stands steadfast and calm, ready to welcome all who will turn to Him and accept the blessings of safety and peace. For we are living in an age of grace, in which God promises that whosoever will may come and receive His Son. But this period of grace will not go on indefinitely. We are even now living on borrowed time.

2

The Indestructible Bible

Heaven and earth shall pass away, but my words shall not pass away.

Matthew 24:35

TIME is running out. The seconds are ticking away toward midnight. The human race is about to take the fatal plunge. Have we just been placed here by some unknown creator or force without any clue as to where we came from, why we are here, and where we are going? Which way shall we turn? Is there any authority left? Is there a path we can follow? Is there any light penetrating the inky darkness? Can we find a codebook that will give us the key to our dilemmas? Is there any source of authority to which we can turn?

The answer to the first question is, No. The answer to all the rest is, Yes. We do have a codebook. We do have a key. We do have authoritative source material. It is found in the ancient and historic Book we call the Bible. This Book has come down to us through the ages. It has passed through so many hands, appeared in so many forms—and survived attack of every kind. Neither barbaric vandalism nor civilized scholarship has touched it. Neither the burning of fire nor the laughter of skepticism has accomplished its annihilation. Through the many dark ages of man, its glorious promises have survived unchanged. It is interesting to note that when Bible reading was outlawed in our public schools it was required reading in the Catholic schools of communist Poland.

The British and Foreign Bible Society was on Jerusalem Street, one of the main streets of Old Warsaw in World War II. When the Germans began bombing the city, the wife of the director went to the storeroom and carried some 2,000 Bibles down to the basement. She was trapped by the bombing and later captured by the Germans and put in a prison camp. She managed to escape and after the war was over was able to get to those 2,000 Bibles and distribute them to people in need. Warsaw was flattened, but on Jerusalem Street one wall of the old British and Foreign Bible Society remained standing. On it were these words, painted in large letters: "HEAVEN AND EARTH SHALL PASS AWAY, BUT MY WORDS SHALL NOT PASS AWAY."

Now, as we approach what appears to be another decisive hour in world history, let us re-examine this indestructible Book of wisdom and prophecy; let us find out why this particular volume has endured and been man's unfailing source of faith and spiritual strength.

The Bible Is More Than Just Great Literature

There are those who regard the Bible principally as the history of Israel. Others admit that it sets forth the soundest ethics ever enunciated. But these things, important as they are, are only incidental to the real theme of the Bible, which is the story of God's redemption as it exists in Jesus Christ. In an editorial which appeared 30 June 1983 the *International Herald Tribune* recommended that the Bible should be read as literature because it is "The English language at its best." Those who read the Scriptures as magnificent literature, breath-taking poetry, or history and overlook the story of salvation miss the Bible's real meaning and message.

God caused the Bible to be written for the express purpose of revealing to man God's plan for his redemption. God caused this Book to be written that He might make His everlasting laws clear to His children and that they might have His great wisdom to guide them and His great love to comfort them as they make their way through life. For without the Bible, this world would indeed be a dark and frightening place, without signpost or beacon.

The Bible easily qualifies as the only Book in which is God's revelation. There are many bibles of different religions; there is the Muslim Koran, the Buddhist Canon of Sacred Scripture, the Zoroastrian Zend-Avesta, and the Brahman Vedas. All of these have been made accessible to us by reliable translations. Anyone can read them, comparing them with the Bible, and judge for themselves. It is soon discovered that all these nonChristian bibles have parts of truth in them, but they are all developments ultimately in the wrong direction. They all begin with some flashes of true light and end in utter darkness. Even the most casual observer soon discovers that the Bible is radically different. It is the only Book that offers man a redemption and points the way out of his dilemmas. It is our one sure guide in an unsure world.

Sixteen hundred years were needed to complete the

writing of the Bible. It is the work of more than thirty authors, each of whom acted as a scribe of God. Those men, many of whom lived generations apart, did not set down merely what they thought or hoped. They acted as channels for God's revelation; they wrote as He directed them; and under His divine inspiration they were able to see the great and enduring truths and to record them that other men might see and know them too.

During these sixteen hundred years, the sixty-six books of the Bible were written by men of different languages, living in different times, and in different countries; but the message they wrote was one. God spoke to each man in his own language, in his own time, but His message basically in each case was the same. When the great scholars gathered together the many ancient manuscripts written in Hebrew, Aramaic, and Greek and translated them into a single modern tongue, they found that God's promises remain unchanged, His great message to man had not varied. As we read these ageless words today, we find that the rules of conduct set forth by the ancient scribes are as fresh and meaningful to this generation as they were to the people of Jesus' time. John Ruskin said: "The Bible is the one Book to which any thoughtful man may go with any honest question of life or destiny and find the answer of God by honest searching."

The World's Bestseller!

It is small wonder, then, that the Bible has always been the world's best seller! No other book can touch its profound wisdom, its poetic beauty, or the accuracy of its history and prophecy.

Its critics, who claimed it to be filled with forgery, fiction, and unfilled promises, are finding that the difficulties lie with themselves, and not the Bible. Greater and more careful scholarship has shown that apparent contradictions were caused by incorrect translations rather than divine inconsistencies. It was man and not the Bible who needed correcting. Someone has said, "The Bible does not have to be rewritten, but reread."

And yet—in many homes and among so-called educated people—it has become fashionable to joke about the Bible and to regard it more as a dust catcher than as the living Word of God. When asked by her minister if she knew what was in the Bible, one little girl proudly replied that she knew everything that was in it and proceeded to list "the picture of her sister's boyfriend, the coupon for mother's favorite hand lotion, a lock of baby brother's hair, and the ticket for Pa's watch!" That was all she knew about the family Bible. Too many families have used the Bible as a safe storage place for old letters and pressed flowers and have overlooked entirely the help and assurance that God intended this Book to give them.

This attitude is changing now, and changing fast! Life is being stripped of its artificialities, its meaningless trimmings. The false promises that man has made to man are standing forth now as the glaring errors they are. As we cast our frightened eyes around for something that is real and true and enduring, we are turning once more to this ancient Book that has given consolation, comfort, and salvation to millions in the centuries past. My wife Ruth once said, "If our children have the background of a godly, happy home and this unshakeable faith that the Bible is indeed the Word of God, they will have a foundation that the forces of hell cannot shake." I thank God for her godly influence in the lives of our children.

Yes, people are "discovering" the Bible again! They are dusting off their old copies or buying new ones. They are finding that the familiar but almost forgotten phrases ring with a current meaning that makes them seem to have been written only yesterday. This is because the Bible embodies all the knowledge man needs to fill the longing of his soul and solve all his problems. It is the blueprint of the Master Architect, and only by following its directions can we build the life we are seeking.

Here in America we have another great document that we value and respect. It was written some 200 years ago by a number of men who labored long and debated even longer over its many provisions and finally sent it to the thirteen federated states for ratification. The men who framed our Constitution knew they were writing the basic document for a government of free men; they recognized that men could live as free and independent beings only if each one knew and understood the law. They were to know their rights, their privileges, and their limitations. They were to stand as equals before the court of law and few judges could be unfair; for the judge, too, was bound by the same law and required to try each case accordingly.

The Truth Shall Set Us Free!

While the rest of the world watched this great human experiment, men found that if they knew the law and lived according to it, they could, in truth, be free! A man could know just where he stood. He had his Constitutional rights, and he also had his Constitutional responsibilities.

If he neglected one, the other would suffer—as so many negligent voters who came later were to discover when they found themselves saddled with governmental restrictions they didn't like!

Just as America has grown and prospered within the framework of our Constitution, so Christianity has flourished and spread according to the laws set forth in the Bible. Just as the Constitution was intended to apply equally to all men living under it, without special favor or interpretation, so the Bible stands as the supreme Constitution for all mankind, its laws applying equally to all who live under its domain, without exception or special interpretation.

As the Constitution is the highest law of the land, so the Bible is the highest law of God. For it is in the Bible that God sets forth His spiritual laws. It is in the Bible that God makes His enduring promises. It is in the Bible that God reveals the plan of redemption for the human race.

In the wonders of nature we see God's laws in operation. Who has not looked up at the stars on a cloudless night and marveled in silent awe at the glory of God's handiwork? Even our astronauts have lauded the Lord as Creator of the vastness of space and the intricacies of our universe which we are just now beginning to explore. If we could not depend on His laws, we could not make these excursions into space. Who has not felt his heart lifted in the spring of the year, as he sees all creation bursting with new life and vigor? In the beauty and abundance around us we see the magnitude of God's power and the infinite detail of His planning; but nature tells us nothing of God's love or God's grace. We do not find the promise of our personal salvation in nature.

Conscience tells us in our innermost being of the presence of God and of the moral difference between good and evil; but this is a fragmentary message, in no way as distinct and comprehensive as the lessons of the Bible. It is only in its pages that we find the clear and unmistakable message upon which all true Christianity is based.

The laws of our land find their genesis in the Ten Commandments. And Sir William Blackstone, the great English jurist, wrote: "The Bible has always been regarded as part of the Common Law of England."

Christianity finds all its doctrines stated in the Bible, and Christianity denies no part, nor attempts to add anything to the Word of God. While the Constitution of the United States may be amended from time to time, no amendment is ever necessary for the Bible. We truly believe that the men who wrote the Bible were guided by the Holy Spirit, both in the thoughts they expressed and in their choice of words. As Peter said, "For the prophecy came not in old time by the will of man: but holy men of God spake as they were moved by the Holy Ghost" (2 Peter 1:21).

Paul tells us that "All scripture is given by inspiration of God, and is profitable for doctrine, for reproof, for correction, for instruction in righteousness: That the man of God may be perfect, thoroughly furnished unto all good works" (2 Timothy 3:16–17).

In setting down their forthright messages, biblical scribes have never attempted to gloss over the realities of life. The sins of the great and small are freely admitted, the weaknesses of human nature are acknowledged, and life in biblical times is recorded as it was lived. The startling thing is that the lives and motivations of these people who lived so long ago have such a modern flavor! As we read, the pages seem like mirrors held up before our own minds and hearts, reflecting our own prides and prejudices, our own failures and humiliations, our own sins and sorrows.

Truth is timeless. Truth does not differ from one age to another, from one people to another, from one geographical location to another. Men's ideas may differ, men's customs may change, men's moral codes may vary, but the great all-prevailing Truth stands for time and eternity.

The message of Jesus Christ, our Savior, is the story of the Bible—it is the story of salvation. Profound students of the Bible have traced the story of Jesus Christ from the beginning of the Old Testament, for He is the true theme of the Old as well as the New Testament.

The fact of Jesus Christ is the eternal message of the Bible. It is the story of life, peace, eternity, and heaven. The Bible has no hidden purpose. It has no need for special interpretation. It has a single, clear, bold message for every living being—the message of Christ and His offer of peace with God.

One day upon a mountain near Capernaum Jesus sat with His disciples. They gathered before Him—perhaps Peter on one side and John on the other. Jesus may have looked quietly and tenderly at each of these devoted disciples, looked at them the way a loving parent looks at the members of his family—loving each child separately, loving each one for a special reason, loving them in such a way that each child feels singled out and individually embraced. That is how Jesus must have loved His disciples.

The little group must have become very reverent under His serene and loving gaze. They must have become very still within themselves with the feeling that something momentous was about to be said, something they must remember, something they must be able to transmit to others all over the world who were not privileged, as they were, to hear these words from the Master's own lips.

For there, on the mountain, standing perhaps under the silvery gray-green leaves of an olive tree, Jesus preached the greatest sermon that human ears have ever heard. He explained the essence of Christian living. When He was through and a holy hush had settled on His wide-eyed listeners, they "were astonished at his doctrine: for he taught them as one having authority, and not as the scribes" (Matthew 7:28, 29).

Indeed He did teach with authority, the authority of God Himself; and the rules He set forth were God's own rules, the ones which every Christian with the hope of salvation in his heart must follow.

You and the Bible

If you do not have a Bible in your home, go out and get one now—get the one that suits you best, get the size that is most comfortable for you to handle, get the kind of type that is most pleasant for you to read, and then settle down and find out for yourself why this one Book has endured. Don't be afraid to invest in the best Bible you can afford—for that is what you are making: an investment. We spend our money for expensive clothing which perishes but hesitate to buy the best in Bibles which is an investment in eternity. Find out for yourself why it answers every human need, why it supplies the faith and strength that keeps humanity marching forward.

If you and the Bible have had a long absence from each other, it might be well for you to renew your acquaintance by reading again the Gospel of John. While this is considered one of the most profound books in the Bible, it is also the clearest and most readily understood. It was written for the very purpose of showing the how and the why of man's salvation, so that the questions of the mind as well as the gropings of the heart might be satisfied.

After reading the Book of John, you might acquaint yourself with the Gospel as taught by Mark, Luke, and Matthew, noting how these men of widely different personalities and writing styles set forth the eternal story of redemption through Jesus. You will become aware of the powerful, universal truth that underlies all gospel teaching and be impressed anew with what the biblical writer meant when he said, "Jesus Christ the same yesterday, and today, and forever" (Hebrews 13:8).

When you have read each of the Gospels individually, start in at the beginning of the New Testament and read straight through all the books in order. When you have done that, you will have developed such a taste for Bible reading, you will have found it such a fountain of inspiration, such a practical counselor and guide, such a treasure chest of sound advice, that you will make Bible reading a part of your daily life.

A knowledge of the Bible is essential to a rich and meaningful life. For the words of this Book have a way of filling in the missing pieces, of bridging the gaps, of turning the tarnished colors of our life to jewel-like brilliance. Learn to take your every problem to the Bible. Within its pages you will find the correct answer.

But most of all, the Bible is a revelation of the nature of

God. The philosophers of the centuries have struggled with the problem of a Supreme Being. Who is He? What is He? Where is He? If there is such a Person, is He interested in me? If so, how can I know Him? These and a thousand other questions about God are revealed in this Holy Book we call the Bible.

A Christian once asked, "Do you know a book that you are willing to put under your head for a pillow when you are dying? Very well," Joseph Cook went on, "that is the Book you want to study when you are living. There is only one such Book in the world!"

3

What Is God Like?

Canst thou by searching find out God?
Job 11:7

WHO is God? What is He like? How can we be sure He exists? When did He begin? Can we know Him?

Everyone has asked these questions either aloud or to himself, for we cannot look at the world around us and not wonder about its creation. We are daily faced with the miracle of life and the mystery of death, of the glory of flowering trees, the magnificence of the star-filled sky, the magnitude of mountains and of sea. Who made all this? Who conceived the law of gravity by which everything is held in its proper place? Who ordered the day and the night and the regular procession of the seasons? What about the infinity of the universe? Can we honestly believe (as someone has written), "This is all there is or was or ever will be"?

The only possible answer is that all these things and many more are the work of a Supreme Creator. As a watch must have a designer, so our precision-like universe has a

Great Designer. We call Him God. His is a name with whom the whole human race is familiar. From earliest childhood we have breathed His name. The Bible declares that the God we talk about, the God we sing about, the God "from whom all blessings flow!" is the God who created this world and placed us in it. Our exploration of space would be impossible in a universe ungoverned by the laws of God.

No less a wise man than Benjamin Franklin said, "I have lived a long time and the longer I live the more convincing proofs I see that God governs in the affairs of men." Another wise man, Blaise Pascal, wrote: "If a man is not made for God, why is he happy only in God? If man is made for God, why is he opposed to God?" This is our dilemma.

But "Who is He?" you ask. "Where is He?" We know that He exists. We call upon Him in our hours of greatest difficulty and trial. Some try to let the thought of Him fill every waking moment. Others say they don't believe in Him, that He doesn't exist. And still others say, "Explain Him to me and maybe I'll accept God."

For those who, at this crucial point in world history, are wondering "What is God like?" it has been simply stated: God is like Jesus Christ. Just as Jesus came to make God visible to mankind and to become our Redeemer, even so, on His return to Heaven, He sent the Holy Spirit to indwell believers and enable them to live so as to make Christ visible to an unbelieving world.

If that is how you feel, if all your life you have been hearing about God and talking about God, but waiting for someone to explain God to you before you could put your faith in Him, and Him alone, let us see just how concrete a description the Bible can give us.

What Is God Like?

At this crucial point in world history, everyone should be seeking an answer to the question, "What is God like?" Everyone should ask it, and everyone should make very sure of the answer. Everyone should know beyond a shadow of a doubt exactly who God is and what He is capable of accomplishing. The Bible says, "Because that which may be known of God is manifest in them; for God hath shewed it unto them" (Romans 1:19).

It is the absence of the knowledge of God and man's refusal to obey Him that lie at the root of every problem which besets us. It is man's confusion about God's plan that has the world in chaos. It is man's unwillingness to learn and to obey God's laws that has laid such a heavy burden on our souls. So let us learn all that we can about Him.

Where shall we go for this knowledge? Who among us can tell us the truth? Are we not all finite creatures here together? Has God designated any one person here on earth to speak with final authority about Him? No—the one Man who could do that lived two thousand years ago, and we crucified Him! How then, are we to find out?

We can ask the learned scholars, and they may tell us that God is the expression of everything in nature and life, that all living beings are one with God, that life itself is an expression of His Divine Being. They will tell you that you can see God in the tiniest drop of water and in the great arch of the sky above.

Ask a philosopher, and he will tell you that God is the original and immutable force behind all creation, that He is the Master Dynamo who keeps all the worlds in motion—that He is the Power without beginning or end. The philosopher will say that every bit of life and beauty we see is a manifestation of this power which flows in an unending current out from the Dynamo and back again.

Ask still further and you may be told that God is absolute, that He is All in All, and that no one can possibly know any more about Him. There are many differing definitions for God. Dr. Akbar Haqq says that *originally* all people were monotheistic in their concept of God. Every country, every race of people, every family, every individual has tried to explain the Great Being behind the universe. Men of all ages have tried to discover the Creator whose work they saw, but whom they did not know. Which of these varied explanations is right? Which of these many theories are we to accept? By which of these self-appointed authorities are we to be guided?

As we have already seen in our previous chapter, God has revealed Himself in the Book called the Bible. In the Bible we have a revelation of God—and based on it our minds can be satisfied and our hearts filled. We can rest assured that we have the correct answer, that we are on our way to knowing and understanding the true nature of God.

God reveals Himself in hundreds of ways in the Bible, and if we read the Bible as carefully and as regularly as we read the daily papers, we would be as familiar with and as well informed about God as we are about our favorite player's batting average during baseball season!

As a diamond has many facets, so there are innumerable aspects of God's revelation of Himself which would take volumes to fill. Suffice it to say, with our limited space we can cover four aspects of God's revelation of Himself which seem to be the most significant, and which we should carry with us always.

'God As Spirit'

First: the Bible declares God to be *Spirit.* Jesus talking to the woman at the Well of Sychar made this straightforward statement about God: "God is Spirit" (John 4:24).

What do you think of when you hear the word *spirit*? What mental image does it bring to your mind? Do you think of a wisp of vapor drifting across the sky? Does *spirit* mean the sort of thing that frightens children on Halloween? Is *spirit* just a formless nothingness to you? Do you think that was what Jesus meant when He said, "God is Spirit"?

To discover what "spirit" really is, and what Jesus meant when He used that particular word, we must turn again in the Bible to the scene where Christ after His resurrection says: "Handle me, and see; for a spirit hath not flesh and bones, as ye see me have" (Luke 24:39). Therefore we can be sure that spirit is *without* body. It is the *opposite* of body. Yet it has being and power. This is difficult for us to understand because we are trying to understand it with our limited, finite minds.

As human beings deprived of the unlimited vision that God originally intended His creatures to have, we cannot comprehend the glory and the magnitude of the Spirit that lies so far outside ourselves. When we hear the word "spirit," we immediately try to reduce it to our puny size, to make it fit within the scope of our small minds. It is like trying to explain the sweep and majesty and awe-inspiring grandeur of the ocean to a person who has never seen a body of water larger than a mud puddle! How can such a person envision the boundless sea? How can such a person, looking into a shallow, murky pool, fathom the bottomless depths, the mysterious life, the surging power, the ceaseless roll, the terrible ruthlessness of ocean storm or the all-surpassing beauty of ocean calm? How could anyone who had looked only into a mud puddle know what you were talking about? What words could you use to describe the mighty sea convincingly? How could you make a person believe that such a wonder really exists?

How infinitely more difficult it is for us to grasp what Jesus meant when He said: "God is Spirit." Jesus knew! His mind was not limited as our minds are limited. His eyes were not focused on the mud puddle of life. He knew full well the borderless reaches of the Spirit, and He came to try to give us some understanding of its wonders, its comfort, and its peace.

We do know that the spirit is not something bound in a body. Spirit is not wearable as a body. Spirit is not changeable as a body. The Bible declares that God is a Spirit—that He is not limited to body; He is not limited to shape; He is not limited to boundaries or bonds; He is absolutely immeasurable and undiscernible by eyes that can see only physical things. The Bible tells us that because He has no such limitations He can be everywhere at once—that He can hear all, see all, and know all.

We can't do any of that, and so we try to limit God as we are limited. We try to deny God the power to do things we can't do. We try to say that because we can't be everywhere at once, God can't be, either! We are rather like the person who, having heard about the ocean, finally makes his way to the beach one day and going down to the edge of the water, scoops up a few drops and holds them in his hands.

"Ah," he exclaims, "at last I have made the ocean mine! I hold the ocean in my hands. I possess it!" True, he does have a part of the ocean, but at the same moment other people on a thousand other shores may be reaching down and claiming a few drops of the ocean for themselves. The world's millions could come down to the beach and reach out their hands to be filled with sea water. They could each take as much as they wanted, as much as they needed—and still the ocean would remain unchanged. Its mightiness and power would be the same; the life in its unfathomable depths would continue unaltered, although it had supplied the needs of every single person standing with outstretched hands along its many shores.

So it is with God. He can be everywhere at once, heeding the prayers of all who call out in the name of Christ; performing the mighty miracles that keep the stars in their places and the plants bursting up through the earth and the fish swimming in the sea. There is no limit to God. There is no limit to His wisdom. There is no limit to His power. There is no limit to His love. There is no limit to His mercy.

If you have been trying to limit God—stop it! Don't try to confine Him or His works to any single place or sphere. You wouldn't try to limit the ocean. You cannot limit the universe. You wouldn't be bold enough to try to change the course of the moon, or to stop the earth as it turns on its axis! How everlastingly more foolish it is to try to limit the God who created and controls all these wonders!

I am eternally grateful to my mother for many things, but one of the most enduring blessings she brought into my life was to teach me in the Catechism at the age of ten that "God is a Spirit, infinite, eternal, and unchangeable in his being, wisdom, power, holiness, justice, goodness, and truth." That definition of God has been with me all my life, and when a man knows in his heart that God is an infinite, eternal, and unchangeable Spirit, it helps to overcome the temptation to limit Him. It helps to overcome all doubt about His ability to accomplish things that we can't do ourselves!

Some who doubt that the Bible is the true Word of God, doubt it because they are unwilling to ascribe to God anything they cannot themselves achieve. If you have any uncertainty about the inspiration of the Bible, go back and look at it again. Look at it in the light of a person who has been staring at a mud puddle all his life and who is confronted for the first time by a view of the ocean! Perhaps you are only now catching your first glimpse of God's unlimited power. Perhaps you are only now beginning to understand Him for what He actually is. For if God is the Spirit that Jesus declares Him to be, there is no problem of providence, there is no problem of His sovereignty in the affairs of men, there is no problem of His inspiration of the men who wrote the Bible. Everything fits into place once you understand who and what God really is.

God Is a Person

Second: the Bible reveals Him as a *Person*. All through the Bible it says: "God loves," "God says," "God does." Everything that we attribute to a person is attributed to God. A person is one who feels, thinks, wishes, desires, and has all the expressions of personality.

Here on earth we confine personality to the body. Our finite minds cannot envision personality that is not manifested through flesh and bones. We know that our own personalities will not always be clothed in the bodies they now inhabit. We know that at the moment of death our personalities will leave our bodies and go on to the destinations that await them. We know all this—yet it is difficult for us to accept it.

What a revelation if we could all realize that personality does not have to be identified with a physical being. God is not bound by a body, yet He is a Person. He feels, He thinks, He loves, He forgives, He sympathizes with the problems and sorrows that we face.

God is Holy and Righteous

Third: the Bible states that God is not only a Spirit and a Person, but God is also a *Holy and Righteous Being.* From Genesis to Revelation, God reveals Himself as a Holy God. He is utterly perfect and absolute in every detail. He is too holy to tolerate sinful man, too holy to endure sinful living.

If we could envision the true picture of His majestic righteousness, what a difference it would make in the way we live as individuals and as nations! If we could but realize the tremendous gulf that separates unrighteous man from God's perfect righteousness! The Scripture declares Him to be the Light in whom there is no darkness at all—the one Supreme Being without flaw or blemish.

Here again is a difficult concept for imperfect man to understand. We, whose faults and weaknesses are everywhere apparent, can scarcely imagine the overwhelming holiness of God—but we must recognize it if we are to understand and benefit from the Bible.

The chasm that separates imperfect man from perfect God is emphasized all through the Scriptures. We see it in the division of the Old Testament Tabernacle and the New Testament Temple into the Holy and Most Holy places. It is pointed out in the prescribed offering that must be brought if a sinner would approach God. It is underscored by a special priesthood to mediate between God and the people. It is emphasized by the laws concerning impurity in the Book of Leviticus. We see it in the many feasts of Israel, by the isolation of Israel in Palestine. The Holiness of God regulates all other principles of God.

The Scripture declares that His throne is established on the basis of His holiness. It is because God is holy and man is unholy that so wide a rift exists between God and the unrepentant sinner. The Bible tells us that our iniquities have separated us from God—separated us so completely that His face is hidden from us and He will not hear us when we call. "If I regard iniquity in my heart," says the psalmist, "the Lord will not hear me" (Psalm 66:18). On the other hand, the psalmist says, "The eyes of the Lord are upon the righteous, and his ears are open unto their cry . . . The Lord . . . will fulfill the desire of them that fear him: he also will hear their cry, and will save them" (Psalms 34:15; 145:18, 19).

God is too pure to look with approval upon evil, which means that He is too holy to have any dealings with sin. Before sin entered into the human race, God and man had fellowship with each other. Now that fellowship is broken, and all communication between God and man is lost outside of Jesus Christ. It is only through Jesus Christ that man can ever again re-establish His fellowship with God. There are those who say that all roads lead to God. But Jesus said, "I am *the way, the truth, and the life*, no man cometh unto the Father but by me" (John 14:6). He also said, "I am the door: by me if any man enter in, he shall be saved, and shall go in and out, and find pasture" (John 10:9).

Man is a sinner, powerless to change his position, powerless to reach the pure ear of God unless he cries out for mercy sincerely. Man would have remained forever lost if God in His infinite mercy had not sent His Son to earth to bridge this gulf.

It is in God's holiness that we find the reason for the death of Christ. Jesus was the only one good enough, pure enough, strong enough, to bear the sins of the whole world. God's holiness demanded the most exacting penalty for sin, and His love provided Jesus Christ to pay this penalty and provide man with salvation. Because the God we worship is a pure God, a holy God, a just and righteous God, He sent us His only begotten Son to make it possible for us to have access to Him. But if we ignore the help He has sent, if we fail to obey the laws He has set forth, we cannot cry out to Him for mercy when the punishment we deserve falls upon us!

'God Is Love'

Fourth: God is *Love*. But as with the other attributes of God, many persons who do not read their Bibles fail to recognize what is meant when the Scriptures say: "God is love" (1 John 4:8).

We aren't always sure ourselves what we mean when we use the term *love*. That word has become one of the most widely misused words in our language. We use the word *love* to describe the basest as well as the most exalted of human relationships. We say we "love" to travel; we "love" to eat chocolate cake; we "love" our new car, or the pattern in the wallpaper in our home. Why, we even say we "love" our neighbors—but most of us don't do much more than just say it and let it go at that! No wonder we don't have a very clear idea of what the Bible means when it says: "God is Love."

Don't make the mistake of thinking that because God is Love everything is going to be sweet, beautiful, and happy and that no one will be punished for his sins. God's holiness demands that all sin be punished, but God's love provides the plan and way of redemption for sinful man. God's love provided the cross of Jesus, by which man can have forgiveness and cleansing. It was the love of God that sent Jesus Christ to the cross!

Never question God's great love, for it is as unchangeable a part of God as is His holiness. No matter how terrible your sins, God loves you. Were it not for the love of God, none of us would ever have a chance in the future life. But God is Love! And His love for us is everlasting! "But God commendeth his love toward us, in that while we were yet sinners, Christ died for us" (Romans 5:8).

The promises of God's love and forgiveness are as real, as sure, as positive as human words can make them. But like describing the ocean, its total beauty cannot be understood until it is actually seen. It is the same with God's love. Until you actually accept it, until you actually experience it, until you actually possess true peace with God, no one can describe its wonders to you.

It is not something that you do with your mind. Your finite mind is not capable of dealing with anything as great as the love of God. Your mind might have difficulty explaining how a black cow can eat green grass and give white milk—but you drink the milk and are nourished by it. Your mind can't reason through all the intricate processes that take place when you plant a small flat seed that produces a huge vine bearing luscious red and green watermelons—but you eat them and enjoy them! You can't understand radio, but you listen. Your mind can't explain the electricity that may be creating the light by which you are reading at this very moment—but you know that it's there and that it is making it possible for you to read!

You have to receive God by faith—by faith in His Son, the Lord Jesus Christ. And when that happens, there isn't any room for doubt. You don't have to question whether or not God is in your heart; you can know it.

Whenever anyone asks me how I can be so certain about who and what God really is, I am reminded of the story of the little boy who was out flying a kite. It was a fine day for kite flying; the wind was brisk and large billowy clouds were blowing across the sky. The kite went up and up until it was entirely hidden by the clouds.

"What are you doing?" a man asked the little boy.

"I'm flying a kite," he replied.

"Flying a kite, are you?" the man said. "How can you be sure? You can't see your kite."

"No," said the boy, "I can't see it, but every little while I feel a tug, so I know for sure that it's there!"

Don't take anyone else's word for God. Find Him for yourself, and then you too will know by the wonderful, warm tug on your heartstrings that He is there *for sure.*

4

The Terrible Fact of Sin

For all have sinned, and come short of the glory of God.

Romans 3:23

IF GOD is a righteous and loving Being, why then is there so much wickedness, suffering, and sorrow? How did all this hatred come to be? Why have we created false idols? Why do we worship at the shrines of greed, self-interest, and war? How did the human race, which God made in His own image, sink so deep into depravity that the Ten Commandments had to be set forth with the demand that they be kept? Why did God have to send His own Son to save us? How did God's creatures become so filled with lust and evil?

To understand it, to see clearly why nation is pitted against nation, why families are divided, why every newspaper is filled with reports of violent, insane acts of brutality and hatred, we must go back to the very beginning. We must go back to the story of Adam in the Garden, back to the first chapter of Genesis.

Some people say that this familiar story of creation is only a myth. They say it is but a simple way to explain an unanswerable question to children. But this is not so. The Bible tells us exactly what happened in the beginning and why man has moved steadily along the path of his own destruction ever since.

For God created this world as a perfect whole. He created the beautiful, harmonious world that man threw away—the perfect world that we are longing to find again, the world for which we are all searching.

In this perfect world God placed a perfect man. Adam was perfect because nothing that God does can ever be less than perfect, and upon this perfect man God bestowed not only the most precious gift of all—the gift of life eternal. He also gave him the gift of freedom. God gave to man the freedom of choice.

A friend of ours, Dr. M. L. Scott, the great black preacher, tells about a friend of his. The friend's son had gone away to the university for study and returned home for a visit, filled with his newly acquired knowledge.

"Dad," he said one evening with vast importance, "now that I've been to university, I'm no longer sure I can go along with your simple, childlike faith in the Bible."

The friend sat there studying his son with unblinking eyes. Finally he said, "Son, that is your freedom—your terrible freedom." That is what God gave to Adam—his freedom to choose. His terrible freedom.

The first man was no cave dweller—no gibbering, grunting, growling creature of the forest trying to subdue the perils of the jungle and the beasts of the field. Adam was created fullgrown with every mental and physical faculty developed. He walked with God and had fellowship with Him. He was intended to be as a king on earth, ruling by the will of God.

This, then, was Adam's position as he stood in the Garden, the perfect man, the first man, with his priceless, if terrible gift of freedom. Adam had *total* freedom—freedom to choose or to reject, freedom to obey God's commands or to go contrary to them, freedom to make himself happy or miserable. For it is not the mere possession of freedom that makes life satisfying—it is what we choose to *do* with our freedom that determines whether or not we shall find peace with God and with ourselves.

The Heart of the Problem

This is the real heart of the problem, for the moment a man is given freedom he is faced by two paths. Freedom is meaningless if there is only one possible path to follow. Freedom implies the right to choose, to select, to determine one's individual course of action.

We all know men and women who are honest, not so much from free choice, but because they have no opportunity to be dishonest. Dr. Manfred Gutzke has said, "You old people, don't think you are becoming better just because you are becoming deader." We all know people who pride themselves on being good, when it is actually their surroundings and way of life that keep them from being bad. We cannot take credit for resisting temptation if no temptation is placed before us!

God gave Adam no such handicap. He granted him freedom of choice and He gave him every opportunity to exercise it. Because God could do nothing that was less than perfect, He provided Adam with the perfect setting in which to prove whether or not he would serve God.

As Adam stood there in the Garden he was without sin,

his innocence was without blemish. The whole universe lay before him. The as yet unwritten history of the human race stretched like a great sheet of purest parchment beneath his hand, waiting for him to write the opening chapter—waiting for him to determine which road future generations would take.

God had completed His work. He had created an earthly garden, rich in everything that man might need. He had created a perfect man in His own likeness. He had endowed this man with a mind and a soul, and given him complete freedom to use his mind and to dispose of his soul as he saw fit. Then, like the wise Parent that He was, God waited to see what choice this child of His would make.

The Choice Man Made

This was the test! This was the moment when Adam would use his free will to choose the right path or the wrong path—choose it because he wanted to, and not because there was only one path open to him!

Adam made his choice. He suffered the consequences of it, and he set the pattern that all humanity was to follow. "Therefore, as by the offense of one, judgment came upon all men to condemnation" (Romans 5:18). Paul also says, "Wherefore, as by one man sin entered into the world, and death by sin; and so death passed upon all men, for that all have sinned" (Romans 5:12).

For Adam was the fountainhead of the human race. He sprang like a crystal-clear spring from the ground, and was permitted to choose whether he would become a river running through pleasant and productive green pastures, or a muddy torrent forever dashing against rocks and churning between deep, sunless cliffs—cold and miserable in itself and unable to bring joy and fruitfulness to the surrounding land.

God is not to blame for the tragic snarl in which the world has so long found itself. The fault lies squarely with Adam—Adam who was given his choice and who chose to listen to the lies of the Tempter rather than to the truth of God! The history of the human race from that day to this has been the story of man's futile effort to gain back the position that was lost by Adam's fall and, failing that, to reverse the curse.

"But this is unfair!" you may say. "Why should we suffer today because the first man sinned away back in the furthest reaches of time? Why hasn't mankind recovered during the intervening years? Why should we go on being punished every day of our lives?" There is a thought current today that it is possible to improve man by improving his environment. Isn't it strange to recognize that the first sin was committed in the perfect environment?

Let us turn again to the story of the river—the cold, dark river that runs at the bottom of the deep, dreary gorge. Why doesn't this river make its way back up to the warm, pleasant fields that lie above it? Why doesn't it leave its mournful route and become the happy, bubbling stream it was when it burst spontaneously from the earth?

It doesn't, because it *can't*. It has no power within itself to do other than it has always done. Once it has plunged down the steep banks into darkness, it cannot lift itself again to the bright, sunny land above. The means by which it could be lifted exists, the way is at hand, but the river does not understand how to make use of it. This reminds me of the

Yangtze River in China (now called the Chiang Jiang). This river spews its mud for miles out to sea, turning the blue-green waters of the ocean to a murky yellow. It is helpless to do otherwise.

A miracle stands ever ready to bring the river of humanity out of its misery and to place it once more in the warm valley of peace, but the river doesn't see or heed it. It feels that it can do nothing but continue on its tortuous way until it finally loses itself in the sea of destruction.

The story of the river is the story of man since the time of Adam, winding, twisting, plunging ever deeper into the frightening darkness. Though we lift up our voices and cry out for help, still we deliberately choose—as Adam did—the wrong way. In our despair we turn against God and blame Him for our dilemma. We question His wisdom and judgment. We find fault with His mercy and love.

We forget that Adam was the head of the human race, even as in this country our president is the head of our government. When the president acts, it is really the American people acting through him. When the president makes a decision, that decision stands as the decision of the entire people.

Adam stands as the federal head of the human race. He is also our first forefather. Just as we inherit characteristics, such as intellect, coloring, body size, temperament, etc., from our parents and grandparents, mankind inherited its fallen, corrupt nature from Adam. When he failed, when he succumbed to temptation and fell, the generations yet unborn fell with him, for the Bible states very clearly that the results of Adam's sin shall be visited upon every one of his descendants. We know all too well the bitter truth of those passages in Genesis 3:17–19, which describe the tragedy that Adam's act brought upon us all: "Cursed is the ground for thy sake, in sorrow shalt thou eat of it all the days of thy life; Thorns also and thistles shall it bring forth to thee; and thou shalt eat the herb of the field; In the sweat of thy face shalt thou eat bread, till thou return unto the ground; for out of it wast thou taken: for dust thou art, and unto dust shalt thou return."

And to Eve, God said: "I will greatly multiply thy sorrow and thy conception; in sorrow thou shalt bring forth children; and thy desire shall be to thy husband, and he shall rule over thee" (Genesis 3:16).

In other words, because of Adam's original sin, the ground which once bore only beautiful and nourishing plants now produces both good and bad alike. Man, who once had but to walk in the Garden and reach out his hand for food, who had no need for clothing or for shelter, must now toil all the days of his life to provide these necessities for himself and his family. Woman, once the most carefree of creatures, is now burdened with sorrow and pain; and both man and woman are under penalty of spiritual and physical death. Death is a threefold circumstance: 1) immediate spiritual death; 2) the beginning of physical death (the minute we are born, we begin to die); and 3) ultimate eternal death.

Sin Makes Its Entry

Sin entered the human race through Adam, and the human race has been trying without success to get rid of it ever since. And, short of that, mankind has been seeking in vain to reverse the curse. The Bible teaches that God warned Adam before he sinned that if he ate of the tree of knowledge he would surely die. The Bible also tells us that God instructed Adam and Eve to be fruitful and to multiply and to replenish the earth. But although they had been created in the image of God, after the Fall Adam and Eve gave birth to children after their own likeness and image. Consequently Cain and Abel were infected with the death-dealing disease of sin, which they inherited from their parents and which has been passed on to every generation since. We are all sinners by inheritance, and try as we will, we cannot escape our birthright.

We have resorted to every means to win back the position that Adam lost. We have tried through education, through philosophy, through religion, through governments to throw off our yoke of depravity and sin. We have sought to accomplish with our sin-limited minds the things that God intended to do with the clear vision that can come only from on high. Our motives have been good and some of our attempts have been commendable, but they have all fallen far, far short of the goal. All our knowledge, all our inventions, all our developments and ambitious plans move us ahead only a very little before we drop back again to the point from which we started. For we are still making the same mistake that Adam made—we are still trying to be king in our own right, and with our own power, instead of obeying God's laws.

Before we label God as unjust or unreasonable for permitting sin to envelop the world, let us look at the situation more carefully. God in His infinite compassion sent His Son to show us the way out of our difficulties. He sent His Son to experience the same temptations that were set before Adam and to triumph over them. Satan tempted Jesus, just as he tempted Adam. Satan offered Jesus power and glory if He would forsake God, just as he offered it to Adam through Eve.

The Choice Christ Made

The great difference was that Jesus Christ resisted the temptation! When the devil showed Him all the kingdoms of the world and promised Him all the glory of them if He would but follow Satan instead of God, our blessed Lord said: "Get thee hence, Satan: for it is written, Thou shalt worship the Lord thy God and him only shalt thou serve" (Matthew 4:10). He completely triumphed over the Tempter to reveal to all peoples of all succeeding generations His sinless character. He is our victory!

In our weakness and because of our depraved nature we have proved to be the true sons of Adam and have followed faithfully in his steps. We may deplore Adam's choice but we still imitate him!

There is not a single day that we do not face the same test that was set before Adam. There is not a day that we do not have a chance to choose between the devil's clever promises and God's sure Word.

We long for the day to come when disappointment, disease, and death will vanish—but there is no possibility of this dream coming true as long as we are the unregenerate sons of Adam. Something must be done about our sins. In succeeding chapters we will see that God has done something about this basic problem of the human race.

From the beginning of time until the present moment, man's ungodly quest for power, his determination to use his gift of free choice for his own selfish ends, has brought him to the brink of doom. The rubble and ruins of many civilizations lie scattered over the earth's surface—mute testimony to man's inability to build a lasting world without God. New rubble, new misery is being created daily, and yet man plunges on his pernicious way.

God, meanwhile, in His infinite understanding and mercy, has looked on, waiting with a patience and compassion that passes all understanding. He waits to offer individual salvation and peace to the ones who will come to His mercy. The same two paths that God set before Adam still lie before us. We are still free to choose. We are living in a period of grace while God withholds the eternal punishment we so justly deserve.

It is the presence of sin that prevents man from being truly happy. It is because of sin that man has never been able to obtain the utopia of which he dreams. Every project, every civilization that he builds ultimately fails and falls into oblivion because man's works are all wrought in unrighteousness. The ruins around us at this moment are eloquent witness to the sin that fills the world.

Cause and Effect

Man seems to have lost sight of the ever-present law of cause and effect that operates on every level of this universe. The effects are plain enough, but the deep-seated, all-prevailing cause seems to be less distinct. Perhaps it is the blight of the modern-day philosophy of "progress" that dims man's vision. Perhaps it is because man is so enamored of this foolish, man-created theory that he clings to the belief the race is advancing slowly but surely toward ultimate perfection.

Many philosophers will even argue that the present

world tragedy is but an incident in the upward march, and they point to other periods in human history when the prospect seemed as bleak and the outcome as hopeless. Philosophers would try to say that the sad conditions through which we are now living are but the birth pangs of a better day! That men are still children groping and stumbling along in the kindergarten of existence, still a long, long way from the mature and sensible beings that they will become centuries hence!

But the Bible makes plain what natural science seems so unwilling to admit—that nature reveals both a Creator and a corrupter. Man blames the Creator for the work of the corrupter. Man forgets that our world is not as God made it. God made the world good. Sin corrupted it. God made man innocent, but sin entered and made him selfish. Every manifestation of evil is the result of basic sin—sin that has remained unchanged since the moment it first entered the human race. It may manifest itself in different ways, but fundamentally it is the same sin that causes an African savage to skulk along a jungle trail awaiting his victim with spear in hand, and a well-trained, educated pilot to fly a jet plane over the same jungle ready to bomb an unsuspecting village.

The two men are separated by centuries of culture. One can be said to be much further "progressed" than the other, one has all the advantages of man-made civilization; while the other is still in the "primitive" state—and yet, are they really so different? Are they not both motivated by fear and distrust of their fellow men? Are both not selfishly bent on achieving their own goals at any cost to their brothers? Is a bomb any less savage or brutal, or more civilized than a naked spear? Can we hope to find a solution to our problems so long as both the most "primitive" and the most "progressive" among us are more eager to kill than to love our neighbors?

All the sorrow, all the bitterness, all the violence, tragedy, heartache, and shame of man's history are summed up in that one little word—sin. Today, the general reaction is "so what?" In fact, there is a definite attempt to popularize and glamorize sin. Our most popular T.V. series are concerned with the *decadent* rich. Our magazine covers frequently feature the immoral, the perverted, the psychologically sick. Sin is "in." People don't like to be told they are sinners, even as their parents and grandparents were sinners before them! Yet the Bible declares, "There is no difference: for all have sinned, and come short of the glory of God" (Romans 3:22–23). The Bible declares that every person on earth is a sinner in the sight of God; and whenever I hear anyone take exception to so strong a statement, I am reminded of the story of the church officer who came to talk to the minister one day about sin. He said to the minister, "Doctor, we of the congregation wish you wouldn't talk quite so much or so plainly about sin. We feel that if our boys and girls hear you discuss the subject so much they will all the more easily become sinners. Why don't you call it a 'mistake' or say that our young people are often guilty of using 'poor judgment'—but please don't talk so openly about sin." The minister walked over and took down a bottle of poison from a high shelf and showed it to his visitor. The bottle was plainly marked in big red letters, "Poison! Do not touch!" "What would you have me do?" asked the minister. "Do you feel it would be wise for me to remove this label and put on one that reads 'Essence of Peppermint'? Don't you see that the milder you make the label, the more dangerous you make the poison?"

Sin—plain, old-fashioned sin, the selfsame sin which caused Adam's downfall—is what we are all suffering from today, and it will do us far more harm than good to try to dress it up with a fancy, more attractive label. We don't need a new word for it. What we need is to find out what the word we already have means! Because, although sin is certainly prevalent in the world today, however popularized, however glamorized, there are multitudes of people who are wholly ignorant of its real meaning. It is the misguided, shortsighted view of sin that stands in the way of conversion for many men and women. It is the lack of real understanding of sin that keeps many Christians from living the true life of Christ.

The old spiritual says, "Everybody talkin' 'bout heaven, ain't going there," and the same thing is true of sin. Everybody who talks about sin doesn't have a clear realization of what it means, and it is of supreme importance that we become familiar with how God looks at sin.

We may try to take a light view of sin and to refer to it as "human weakness." We may try to call it a trifle, but God calls it a tragedy. We would pass it off as an accident, but God declares it is an abomination. Man seeks to excuse himself of sin, but God seeks to convict him of it and to save him from it. Sin is no amusing toy—it is a terror to be shunned! Learn, then, what constitutes sin in the eyes of God!

Dr. Richard Beal gives us five words for sin.

First: sin is *lawlessness,* the transgression of the law of God (1 John 3:4). God established the boundary line between good and evil, and whenever we overstep that boundary, whenever we are guilty of intrusion into the forbidden area of evil, we are breaking the law. Whenever we fail to live up to the Ten Commandments, whenever we go contrary to the precepts of the Sermon on the Mount, we have transgressed the law of God and are guilty of sin.

If you look at the Ten Commandments one by one, you will note how today mankind is deliberately, it seems, not only breaking them, but glamorizing the breaking! From idolatry, which is anything we put before God, to remembering the Sabbath day to keep it holy (where would professional baseball and football be if Christians refused to watch them on Sunday?), to honoring parents (books like *Mommie Dearest* that expose the sins of parents), to covetousness, to adultery—it appcars there has been a concerted effort to deliberately break each Commandment. And not only that, but there seems to be a deliberate attempt to make it attractive to do so!

James made it plain that we are all guilty when he said: "But every man is tempted, when he is drawn away of his own lust, and enticed. Then when lust hath conceived, it bringeth forth sin: and sin, when it is finished, bringeth forth death" (James 1:14–15). It is because we have all broken God's laws, all transgressed His commands, that we are all classified as sinners.

Second: the Bible describes sin as *iniquity*. Iniquity is the deviation from right, whether or not the particular act has been expressly forbidden. Iniquity has to do with our inner motivations, the very things that we so often try to keep hidden from the eyes of men and God. They are the wrongs which spring from our own corrupt nature rather than the evil acts which force of circumstances sometimes cause us to commit.

Jesus described this inner corruptness when He said: "From within, out of the heart of men, proceed evil thoughts, adulteries, fornications, murders, thefts, covetousness, wickedness, deceit, lasciviousness, an evil eye, blasphemy, pride, foolishness: All these evil things come from within, and defile the man" (Mark 7:21–23).

Third: the Bible defines sin as *missing the mark*, falling short of the goal that has been set. God's goal is Christ. The object and end purpose of all of life is to live up to the life of Christ. He came to show us what it is possible for man to achieve here on earth; and when we fail to follow His example, we miss the mark and fall short of the divine standard.

Fourth: sin is a form of *trespass*. It is the intrusion of self-will into the sphere of divine authority. Sin is not merely a negative thing, it is not just the absence of love for God. Sin is the making of a positive choice, the preference for self instead of God. It is the centering of affection in one's own being instead of reaching out with all one's heart to embrace God. Egoism and selfishness are the marks of sin as surely as are theft and murder. Perhaps this is the most subtle and destructive form of sin, for in this form it is so easy to overlook the label on the bottle of poison.

Those who cling to themselves, those who center their entire attention on their own beings, those who regard only their own interests and fight to protect only their own rights—these are sinners as much as the drunkard or harlot.

Jesus said: "What shall it profit a man, if he shall gain the whole world, and lose his own soul?" (Mark 8:36). Translated into modern terms, could we not say, "What shall it profit a man to build a vast industrial empire if he is eaten away by ulcers and can enjoy nothing of life? What shall it profit a dictator though he conquer a hemisphere if he must live in constant fear of an avenger's bullet or an assassin's knife? What shall it profit a parent to bring up children with harsh domination if he is rejected by them later and left to a lonely old age?" Without question, the sin of self is a deadly sin.

Fifth: sin is *unbelief*. Unbelief is a sin because it is an insult to the truthfulness of God. "He that believeth on the Son of God hath the witness in himself. He that believeth not God hath made him a liar because he believeth not the record that God gave of his Son" (1 John 5:10).

It is unbelief that shuts the door to heaven and opens it to hell. It is unbelief that rejects the Word of God and refuses Christ as Savior. It is unbelief that causes men to turn a deaf ear to the gospel and to deny the miracles of Christ.

Sin incurs the penalty of death, and no man has the ability in himself to save himself from sin's penalty or to cleanse his own heart of its corruption. Angels and men cannot atone for sin. It is only in Christ that the remedy for sin can be found. It is only Christ who can save the sinner from the fate that surely awaits him. "For the wages of sin is death" (Romans 6:23). "The soul that sinneth, it shall die" (Ezekiel 18:4). "None of them can by any means redeem his brother, nor give to God a ransom for him" (Psalm 49:7). "Neither their silver nor their gold shall be able to deliver them in the day of the Lord's wrath" (Zephaniah 1:18).

The Only Remedy

Man's only salvation from sin stands on a lonely, barren, skullshaped hill; a thief hangs on one cross, a murderer on another, and between them, a Man with a crown of thorns. Blood flows from His hands and feet, it pours from His side, it drops down His face—while those who stand looking on sneer and mock Him.

And who is this tortured figure, who is this Man whom other men seek to humiliate and kill? He is the Son of God, the Prince of Peace, heaven's own appointed Messenger to the sin-ridden earth. This is He, before whom angels fall down and veil their faces. And yet He hangs bleeding and forsaken upon the cross.

What brought Him to this place of horrors? Who inflicted this hideous torture upon the Man who came to teach us love? You did and I did, for it was for your sin and my sin that Jesus was nailed to the cross. In this immortal moment the human race experienced the darkest reaches of sin, it sank to its lowest depths, it touched its foulest limits. No wonder that the sun could not endure and veiled its face!

As Charles Wesley writes:

And can it be that I should gain
An interest in the Savior's blood?
Died He for me, who caused His pain? . . .

Amazing love! how can it be
That Thou, my God, shouldst die for me?

But sin overreached itself on the cross. Man's hideous injustice that crucified Christ became the means that opened the way for man to become free. Sin's masterpiece of shame and hate became God's masterpiece of mercy and forgiveness. Through the death of Christ upon the cross, sin itself was crucified for those who believe in Him. Sin was conquered on the cross. His death is the foundation of our hope, the promise of our triumph! Christ bore in His own body on the tree the sins that shackle us. He died for us and rose again. He proved the truth of all God's promises to man; and if you will accept Christ by faith today, you, too, can be forgiven for your sins. You can stand secure and free in the knowledge that through the love of Christ your soul is cleansed of sin and saved from damnation.

5

Dealing with the Devil

For we wrestle not against flesh and blood,
but against principalities, against powers,
against rulers of the darkness of this world,
against spiritual wickedness in high places.
Ephesians 6:12

THERE is a satanic principle involved in all that is happening today. The Bible describes "that old serpent, called the Devil and Satan, which deceiveth the whole world" (Revelation 12:9), and we know him to be at work confusing all peoples and all nations. His handiwork is to be seen at every turn.

While we would like to take hope that universal peace is drawing closer, it appears instead that we are standing on the brink of Armageddon. We are told that there were hundreds of "little" wars between 1945 and 1979 which caused between twelve and thirteen million deaths. For Satan is determined that the dark, joyless river of humanity shall continue on its tormented way until the end of time. He won over Adam in the Garden, and he is convinced that he can claim the souls of Adam's descendants for himself.

There is not a thinking person in the world today who has not wondered many times about the existence of the devil. That he *does* exist, there is no doubt. We see his power and influence everywhere. The question is not is there a devil, but *how* and *why* did the devil come to be?

We know from the story of Adam and Eve that the devil was already present on earth before God made the first man. Evil already existed, else God would not have made a tree whose fruit gave the awareness of good and bad. There would have been no necessity for such a tree, no possibility of it, if evil had not already been present and man been in need of protection from it.

Did God Create Evil?

Here we face the greatest of all mysteries, the most significant of all secrets, the most unanswerable of all questions. How could God—who is all-powerful, all-holy, and all-loving—have created evil, or permitted the devil to create it? Why did Adam have to be tempted? Why didn't God strike the devil dead when he entered the body of the serpent to whisper evil thoughts to Eve?

The Bible gives us a few hints as to what the answer may be. But the Bible also makes it very clear that man is not supposed to know the full answer until God has allowed the devil and all his designs to help work out His own great plan.

Before the fall of Adam, long before Adam even existed, it would appear that God's universe was divided into spheres of influence, each of which was under the supervision and control of an angel or heavenly prince, all of whom were responsible directly to God. Paul tells us of "thrones, governments, princedoms, and authorities" in both the visible and the invisible world (Colossians 1:16; Ephesians 1:21). The Bible makes frequent mention of angels and archangels, showing that there was established order among them, some being more powerful than others.

The devil must have been just such a powerful, heavenly prince, having the earth assigned to him, perhaps, as his special province. Known as Lucifer, the "lightbearer," he must have stood very close to God—so close, in fact, that ambition entered his heart and he determined not to be God's beloved prince, but to place himself on an equal footing with God Himself! Lucifer was not the counterpart of God, but the counterpart of Michael or Gabriel; he was not a fallen god, but a fallen angel.

It was at this moment that the breach appeared in the cosmos. It was at this moment that the universe—which had been all good and all harmonious to God's will—split, and a portion of it set itself in opposition to God. Just as there are today regimes and sects that deny the existence of God or defy His authority, the devil defied God and attempted to set up his own authority. He abandoned his own position in the government of God and descended into the lower heavens and cried out that he would be like the Most High God. He had been set by God as the prince of this world; and God has not yet removed him from that position, though the righteous basis for that removal has been laid by the death of Christ. Ever since that moment, the devil has been contesting God on earth.

The Devil's Kingdom

As a mighty prince, with hosts of angels at his command, he has set up his kingdom on earth. His power and position here are the very reasons that the Scriptures came to be written. Had Satan not defied God and attempted to rival His power and authority, the story of Adam in the Garden would have been very different. Had Satan not set himself in opposition to God, there would have been no need to give mankind the Ten Commandments, there would have been no need for God to send His Son to the cross.

Jesus and His apostles were well aware of the devil. Matthew records an actual conversation between Jesus and the devil (Matthew 4:1–10). The devil was very real to the Pharisees—so real, in fact, that they accused Jesus of being the devil himself (Matthew 12:24)! There was no doubt in Jesus' mind of the existence of the devil, nor of the power that he wields here on earth.

The devil's strength is clearly demonstrated in the passage from Jude 9 which relates: "Yet Michael the archangel, when contending with the devil he disputed about the body of Moses, durst not bring against him a railing accusation, but said, The Lord rebuke thee."

Modern confusion about the personality of the devil has resulted in large measure from the caricatures of him which became popular during the Middle Ages. To allay their fear of the devil, people tried to laugh at him and pictured him as a foolish, grotesque creature with horns and a long tail. They put a pitchfork in his hand and a feeble-minded leer on his face, and then said to themselves, "Who's afraid of a ridiculous figure like this?"

The truth is that the devil is a creature of vastly superior intelligence, a mighty and gifted spirit of infinite resourcefulness. We forget that the devil was perhaps the greatest and most exalted of all God's angels. He was a sublime figure, who decided to use his divine endowments for his own aims instead of God's. His reasoning is brilliant, his plans ingenious, his logic well nigh irrefutable. God's mighty adversary is no bungling creature with horns and tail—he is a prince of lofty stature, of unlimited craft and cunning, able to take advantage of every opportunity that presents itself, able to turn every situation to his own advantage. He is unrelenting and cruel. He is not, however, all-powerful, omniscient, or omnipresent.

The devil is quite capable of bringing forth the false prophet of which the Bible warns. Upon the wreckage of disbelief and faltering faith the devil will set his masterpiece, the counterfeit king. He will create a religion without a Redeemer. He will build a church without a Christ. He will call for worship without the Word of God.

The Apostle Paul predicted this when he said: "But I fear, lest by any means, as the serpent beguiled Eve through his subtlety, so your minds should be corrupted from the simplicity that is Christ. For if he that cometh preacheth another Jesus, whom we have not preached, or if ye receive another spirit, which ye have not received, or another gospel, which ye have not accepted, ye might well bear with him . . . For such are false apostles, deceitful workers, transforming themselves into the apostles of Christ" (2 Corinthians 11:3, 4, 13).

The Devil and the Anti-Christ

We know that the anti-Christ will appear and try to ensnare the minds and hearts of men. The time draws close, the stage is set—confusion, panic, and fear are abroad. The signs of the false prophet are everywhere at hand, and many may be the living witnesses of the awesome moment when the final act of this age-old drama begins. It may well come in our time, for the tempo is speeding up, events move more swiftly, and on every side we see men and women consciously or unconsciously choosing up sides—aligning themselves with the devil or with God.

It will be a battle to the death, in the truest meaning of that word—a battle that will give no quarter, that will make no allowances or exceptions. The human phase of this battle started in the Garden of Eden when the devil seduced mankind from God, making it possible for there to be billions of warring wills, every man turning to his own way. "All we like sheep have gone astray; we have turned every one to his own way; and the Lord hath laid on him [Christ] the iniquity of us all" (Isaiah 53:6). It will continue until the end of time, until one or the other of these two mighty forces—the force of good or evil—triumphs and places the True King or the false king on the throne.

At this moment in history, two mighty trinities stand face to face: the Trinity of God (the Father, Son, and Holy Ghost) and the false trinity that Satan would have us worship in its place. The trinity of evil (the devil, anti-Christ, and false prophet) is described in the Book of Revelation: "And I saw three unclean spirits like frogs come out of the dragon, and out of the mouth of the beast, and out of the mouth of the false prophet" (Revelation 16:13).

Never for a second of your waking or sleeping life are you without the influence of these two powerful forces, never is there a moment when you cannot deliberately choose to go with one or the other. Always the devil is standing at your side tempting, coaxing, threatening, cajoling. And always on your other side stands Jesus, the all-loving, the all-forgiving, waiting for you to turn to Him and ask His aid, waiting to give you supernatural power to resist the Evil one. You belong to one or the other. There isn't a no-man's land in between where you can hide.

In moments of your greatest fear and anxiety, in moments when you feel yourself helpless in the grip of events you cannot control, when despair and disappointment overwhelm you—in these moments many times it is the devil who is trying to catch you at your weakest point and push you further along the path that Adam took.

In these perilous moments remember that Christ has not deserted you. He has not left you defenseless. As He triumphed over Satan in His hour of temptation and trial, so He has promised that you, too, can have daily victory over the Tempter. Remember: "Ye are of God . . . and have overcome them: because greater is he that is in you, than he that is in the world" (1 John 4:4).

The same Book that tells us over and over again of God's love warns us constantly of the devil who would come between us and God, the devil who is ever waiting to ensnare men's souls. "Be sober, be vigilant; because your adversary the devil, as a roaring lion, walketh about, seeking whom he may devour" (1 Peter 5:8). The Bible describes a personal devil who controls a host of demon spirits that attempt to dominate and control all human activity, "The prince of the power of the air, the spirit that now worketh in the children of disobedience" (Ephesians 2:2).

Don't Doubt the Devil

Don't doubt for a moment the existence of the devil! He is very personal and he is very real! And he is extremely clever! Perhaps the cleverest thing that he has ever done is to convince people he does not exist. Look again at the front page of today's newspaper if you have any question about the personality of the devil. Switch on your local radio or television news commentator. Note the local theater listings, glance at the magazine stands and book racks—in short, just look around you if you feel you need concrete evidence!

Would sane, thinking men and women behave in this way if they were not in the grip of evil? Could hearts filled only with God's love and God's goodness conceive and carry out the acts of violence and malice that are reported to us every day? Could men of education, intelligence, and honest intent gather around a world conference table and fail so completely to understand each other's needs and goals if their thinking was not being deliberately clouded and corrupted?

Whenever I hear an "enlightened" person of our time take issue with the plausibility of a personal, individualized devil in command of a host of evil spirits, I am reminded of this poem by Alfred J. Hough:

Men don't believe in the Devil now, as their fathers used
to do;
They've forced the door of the broadest creed to let his
majesty through.
There isn't a print of his cloven foot or fiery dart from
his brow
To be found on earth or air today, for the world has
voted it so.
Who dogs the steps of the toiling saint and digs the pits
for his feet?

Who sows the tares in the fields of time whenever God
sows the wheat?
The Devil is voted not to be, and of course, the thing is
true;
But who is doing the kind of work that the Devil alone
can do?
We are told that he doesn't go about as a roaring lion
now;
But whom shall we hold responsible for the everlasting
row
To be heard in home, in church and state, to the earth's
remotest bound,
If the Devil by unanimous vote is nowhere to be found?
Won't someone step to the front forthwith and make
their bow and show
How the frauds and crimes of a single day spring up?
We want to know!
The Devil was fairly voted out, and of course, the
Devil's gone;
But simple people would like to know who carries the
business on.

Who, indeed, is responsible for the infamy, terror, and agony that we see all around us? How can we account for the sufferings that we all experience if evil is not a potent force? Modern education has, in truth, impeded our minds. Because of allegedly scientific findings, some have lost their belief in the supernatural powers of Satan, while others worship him.

George Galloway summed up this dubious contribution of current education when he said: "The theory that there is in the universe a power or principle, personal or otherwise, in eternal opposition to God is generally discarded by the modern mind."

The modern mind may discard it, but that doesn't cause the evil principle itself to disappear! Once asked how he overcame the devil, Martin Luther replied, "Well, when he comes knocking upon the door of my heart and asks, 'Who lives here?' the dear Lord Jesus goes to the door and says, 'Martin Luther used to live here but he has moved out. Now I live here.' The Devil, seeing the nail-prints in His hands, and the pierced side, takes flight immediately."

The Certainty of Sin

Sin is certainly a grim fact! It stands like a titanic force, contesting all the good that men may try to accomplish. It stands like a dark shadow, ever ready to blot out whatever light may reach us from on high. We all know this. We all see it. We all are conscious of it in every move we make. Call it what we may, we know of its very real existence. "For we wrestle not against flesh and blood, but against principalities, against powers, against the rulers of the darkness of this world, against spiritual wickedness in high places" (Ephesians 6:12).

How do those who deny the devil and his minions account for the speed with which evil spreads? How do they explain the endless stumbling blocks that are placed in the path of the righteous? How can they reason away the fact that destruction and disaster are but the work of seconds, while construction and rehabilitation are often agonizingly slow?

Breathe a lie into the air, let loose a slanderous tongue—and the words are carried as by magic to the farthest corners. Speak a truth, perform a generous and honest act—and unseen powers will be at work at once to try to hide this tiny ray of light and hope.

When this book was first written thirty years ago no one built churches to the devil, no one constructed pulpits to preach his word. And yet today they do. His word is everywhere, and all too often his word is translated into desperate deeds. If no unseen power is at work corrupting men's hearts and distorting men's thoughts, how can you explain humanity's eagerness to listen to the base and vulgar and vile, while it turns a deaf ear to the good and clean and pure? One has only to listen to the blasphemous words of punk rock to realize that Satan is alive and well on earth.

Would one single person among us ever pass up a piece of ripe delicious fruit to select a rotten piece that was crawling with worms and reeking with decay, if we were not driven to this dreadful choice by a great and sinister power? Yet that is exactly what we all do over and over again. We constantly pass up the rich and beautiful and ennobling experiences and seek out the tawdry, the cheap, and the degrading. These are the works of the devil, and they flourish on every side!

The Struggle Between Good and Evil

What we see happening here on earth is but a reflection of the far greater struggles between good and evil in the unseen realm. We like to think that our planet is the center of the universe, and we attach too much importance to earthly events. In our foolish pride we see with human eyes. But a struggle of infinitely greater magnitude is being waged in the world we cannot see!

The wise men of old knew this. They knew that there is much that the human eye fails to discern and much to which the human ear is deaf. Modern man likes to feel that he "created" radio, television, and computers, that he made it possible to send audible sounds and visible images through space and to make and record impossible amounts of data. The truth is, of course, that these waves, unknown to man, have always existed, and that far greater wonders exist in outer space, of which man may never gain the slightest knowledge. That these wonders were there, the ancient prophets knew—but even they had but a suggestion of their magnitude, even they could catch but the faintest echoes of the mighty battle of the spheres.

One of the many prices Adam paid for listening to the devil was to lose the vision of spiritual dimensions. He lost for himself and all of humanity the capacity for seeing and hearing and understanding anything that was not basely material. Adam closed himself off from the eternal wonders and splendors of the unseen world. He lost the power of true prophecy, the ability to look ahead, and by so doing to better understand and perform the work of the present. He lost his sense of continuity. He became literally "dead in trespasses and sins." He had alienated himself from God.

G. Campbell Morgan says: "Our distance from God is that of inability to know and apprehend the near. It is the distance of the blind man from the glory of the picture in front of him. The distance of the deaf man from the beauty of the symphony sounding round about him. It is the distance of the sensate man from all the movement of life in the midst of which he lives."

But let tragedy or sickness come to us, let us suffer the consequences of our own sins, and we immediately blame God for it! We may be somewhat patient and understanding with our television sets when they do not give us what we want, but we are quick to rail against God and His universe when we get a distorted picture of it.

Let someone get the business promotion we wanted, let someone we consider less deserving succeed where we have failed, and we cry out against God's injustice. We demand to know why God permits such inequalities! We lose sight of the fact that God, like a great master television station, is sending out a perfect image of love and righteousness all the time and that the faulty reception lies with us!

The Evil in Our Eyesight

It is the evil and distortion within ourselves that keeps us from seeing and experiencing God's perfect world. It is our own sin that blurs the image, that keeps us from being God's pure children instead of the children of evil. Paul spoke for all of us when he said: "For the good that I would I do not, but the evil which I would not, that I do" (Romans 7:19). Paul recognized the dreaded enemy, the powerful foe of all mankind, and cried out, "O wretched man that I am! Who shall deliver me from the body of this death? I thank God through Jesus Christ our Lord. So then with the mind I myself serve the law of God; but with the flesh the law of sin" (Romans 7:24–25).

Two overwhelming adversaries were clearly apparent to Paul and he was acutely aware of being torn between their mighty magnetisms. The power of good was pulling his mind and heart toward God, while the power of evil was trying to drag his body down into death and destruction. Two books on demon possession and the rise of the cults might be of interest to you: *Demon Possession,* by John L.

Nevivus (published by Kregel), and *Unholy Devotion: Why Cults Lure Christians,* by Harold L. Bussell (copyright 1983 by The Zondervan Corporation).

You are caught between these same two forces: life and death! Choose God's way, and there is life. Choose Satan's way, and it is death!

6

The Despair of Loneliness

I am forgotten as a dead man out of mind.
I am like a broken vessel.

Psalm 31:12

AFTER the death of her husband, Queen Victoria said, "There is no one left to call me Victoria." Even though she was a queen, she knew what it meant to be lonely.

H. G. Wells said on his sixty-fifth birthday, "I am sixty-five, and I am lonely and have never found peace."

Isadora Duncan, the great ballet dancer who danced before the royalty of Europe and was considered one of the greatest ballet dancers of all time, said, "I have never been alone but that my heart did ache, my eyes fill with tears, and my hands tremble for a peace and a joy that I never found." She went on to say that in the midst of millions of admirers, she was actually a very lonely woman.

A few years ago, a beautiful young Hollywood star with apparently everything a girl could want, ended her life. In the brief note that she left was an incredibly simple explanation—she was unbearably lonely.

The psalmist said, "I am like a pelican of the wilderness:

I am like an owl of the desert. I watch, and am as a sparrow alone upon the house top" (Psalm 102:6).

Again the psalmist said, "Reproach hath broken my heart; and I am full of heaviness: and I looked for some to take pity, but there was none; and for comforters, but I found none" (Psalm 69:20).

The Loneliness of Solitude

First, there is the *Loneliness of Solitude.* I have felt the loneliness of the ocean where there is never a sound except the booming of the surf along rock-strewn shores. I have felt the loneliness of the prairie with only the occasional mournful howl of the coyote. I have felt the loneliness of the mountains broken only by the sighing of the wind.

The sentry standing duty alone at an outpost, the thousands in mental institutions, and those in solitary confinement in prisons and concentration camps know the meaning of the loneliness of solitude.

Louis Zamperini, the great Olympic track star, has told of the terrible loneliness of solitude on a life-raft where he spent forty-eight days during the second World War.

In his fascinating book, *Alone,* Admiral Richard E. Byrd told about the time he spent in bewildering and soul-shattering darkness. He lived alone in a shack that was literally buried in the great glacial icecap that covers the South Pole. He spent five months there. The days were as black as the nights. No living creature of any kind existed within a hundred miles. The cold was so intense that he could hear his breath freeze and crystallize as the wind blew it past his ears.

"At night," he says, "before blowing out the lantern, I formed the habit of planning the morrow's work." He had to, in order to preserve his sanity. "It was wonderful," he continues, "to be able to dole out time in this way. It brought me an extraordinary sense of command over myself; and without constant activity, the days would have been without purpose; and without purpose, they would have ended—as such days always end—in disintegration."

The Loneliness of Society

Probably you think that in that frozen wasteland, Richard Byrd was of all people most lonely. But the *Loneliness of Society* is far worse than the loneliness of solitude, for there is loneliness in great cities far worse than his.

That poor creature living in the dingy tenement who never receives a letter, who never hears one word of encouragement, who never experiences the handclasp of a friend—that wealthy society leader whose money has bought everything but love and happiness—each knows a loneliness few can understand.

There is the loneliness of the street people living in doorways or cardboard boxes, scrounging food in garbage cans—a unique loneliness.

A recent television program showed the demoralizing loneliness of some of our neglected and forgotten old people in dilapidated institutions. The aimless sitting, the vacant eyes, haunted me. They are the living dead. Yet in the background an old derelict, with one finger, was picking out on an equally derelict piano, "What a Friend We Have in Jesus."

In John 5 we read about Jesus as He made His way through the narrow streets of Jerusalem. When He reached the sheepgate by the pool of Bethesda, He observed the great multitudes plagued with various infirmities, waiting to be moved into the water. Suddenly He noticed a poor creature who seemed more needy than all the rest, and tenderly He asked, "Wilt thou be made whole?"

The helpless paralytic looked up and answered, "Sir, I have no man, when the water is troubled, to put me into the pool." Think of it, thirty-eight long, weary years this bundle of pain had been buffeted by the surging human tide of Jerusalem, and after all these years, he must say to Jesus, "Sir, I have no man." He was absolutely friendless.

You can have a friend who sticks closer than a brother. Jesus Christ can make life joyful, satisfying, and glorious to you. All over the world are millions of men and women who love and serve Jesus Christ. The moment you accept Him, you are closer to them than you are to your own blood relatives.

There is not a city in the United States that does not have a warm church to which you could go and meet the most wonderful people in America. There is a giant network of true Christians in every community of America. The moment you clasp their hands, you know that you have friends.

But first, you must repent, surrender, and commit your heart and life to Christ. Let Him forgive your past sins, and He will take you into His family; He will bring you to the hearth, and you will feel the warmth of the fire. If you are lonely today, I beg you, come to Christ and know the fellowship that He brings.

The Loneliness of Suffering

Third, there is the *Loneliness of Suffering*. Some years ago we received a letter from a radio listener who for five years had been crippled into a sitting position by arthritis. For five long, weary, painful years she was unable to stretch out or to lie down, yet she wrote, "I have spent many a day alone, but never a lonely day." Why? It was Christ who made the difference. With Christ as your Savior and constant Companion, you, too, although alone, need never be lonely.

You today who are lying on a hospital bed enduring the loneliness of suffering can rest assured that Christ can give you His grace and strength. While you lie there, you can be useful to Him. You can know something of the ministry of intercession, the greatest ministry on earth, as you pray for others.

The Loneliness of Sorrow

Fourth, there is the *Loneliness of Sorrow.* In the eleventh chapter of John we read of Mary and Martha. Their brother Lazarus was dead. Jesus had not yet come. They stood beside the body of their brother and wept.

For you, too, perhaps the world has become a vast cemetery containing but one grave. You have stood in the sick room and watched the one dearer than all the world to you slip beyond your reach. You crave fellowship.

You want someone to come along with a strong hand to help wipe the tears away, put the smile back on your face, and give you joy through the sorrow. Jesus can do just that. The Bible says, "Casting all your care upon him, for he careth for you" (1 Peter 5:7). God loves His children. If you are willing to trust Him and give yourself to Him, He can carry your sorrow.

The Loneliness of Sin

Fifth, there is the *Loneliness of Sin.* In John 13 we find the story of the Last Supper. Jesus prophesied the betrayal of Judas. In amazement the innocent disciples looked at one another. John asked, "Lord, who is it?" And Jesus said, "He it is, to whom I shall give bread when I have dipped it." And when He had dipped the bread, He gave it to Judas Iscariot, the son of Simon, and then we are told that Satan entered into Judas. Immediately Jesus said, "That thou doest, do quickly." And the Bible says, "He then, having received the bread, went immediately out, and it was night." He went out—out from the presence of Christ—and it was night.

Perhaps you at one time thought you knew the joy and peace of being born into God's family. You experienced the sweet fellowship of God's people. You tasted the complete happiness and satisfaction of Christ's presence with you, but you sinned. You went out from the presence of Christ, and you have found that it is night. You have neither the fellowship of Christians nor the fellowship of sinners, and certainly you no longer have the fellowship of Christ. Perhaps there is no loneliness quite so bitter as the loneliness of a backslidden Christian.

Yet there is forgiveness for you. As you confess and forsake your sins, your fellowship with Christ will be restored. "If we confess our sins, he is faithful and just to forgive us our sins, and to cleanse us from all unrighteousness" (1 John 1:9).

Perhaps you say you are having a pretty good time sinning— and you well may. The Bible says there is a certain pleasure in sin. However, it is short lived and fatal. Perhaps you have read Dr. Kinsey's report or some other survey and are finding a certain satisfaction in knowing how many sinners there are who are as bad as—or worse than—you. You're not alone. No. You're in the vast majority. Where then, you ask, does the loneliness of sin come in? You may be one of a crowd now, but the day is *coming* when each one of you must stand *alone* before Almighty God and be judged. That will be for you the climax of all the loneliness of earth, and but the preview of the loneliness of hell.

For all of these who travel the pathway of sin, there is an engulfing pall of night that isolates them from all good and true fellowship. Sin always has been darkness. Sin always will be darkness. Judas was lonely because of his sin. God says in Hosea 4:17: "Ephraim is joined to idols, let him alone." Because of the covetousness and idolatry of the people of Ephraim, God had said, "Have no fellowship with him, let him completely alone." "All we like sheep have gone astray; we have turned every one to his own way" (Isaiah 53:6). Here again we find the loneliness of sin.

One hour before his fatal duel with Alexander Hamilton, Aaron Burr, sitting in his library at Richmond Hill in New York, wrote to his daughter, "Some very wise man has said, 'O fools, who think it solitude to be alone.'" Already, even before the fatal shot was fired and the bloody deed was done, he felt the loneliness of his sin. In a few hours he was to be a fugitive from the sudden and deep abhorrence of his fellow citizens. His political career was gone forever, and his great ambitions were wrecked.

There are thousands of lonely people in the city and in the country, who carry heavy and difficult burdens of grief, anxiety, pain, and disappointment; but the loneliest soul of all is the man whose life is steeped in sin.

I want to tell you that every sin you deliberately cling to is a mighty power in making you lonely. The older you get, the lonelier you will be. I beg you, come to the foot of the cross and confess that you are a sinner; forsake your sins.

Christ can give you power to overcome every sin and habit in your life. He can break the ropes, fetters, and chains of sin; but you must repent, confess, commit, and surrender yourself to Him first. Right now, it can be settled, and you can know the peace, joy, and fellowship of Christ.

The Loneliness of the Savior

Last, there is the *Loneliness of the Savior.* Thousands of human beings were swarming around Him. There was great joy at the Passover season everywhere, but Jesus was "despised and rejected of men; a man of sorrows and acquainted with grief: and we hid as it were our faces from him; he was despised, and we esteemed him not. Surely he hath borne our griefs, and carried our sorrows: yet we did esteem him stricken, smitten of God, and afflicted. But he was wounded for our transgressions, he was bruised for our iniquities: the chastisement of our peace was upon him; and with his stripes we are healed. All we like sheep have gone astray; we have turned every one to his own way; and the Lord hath laid on him the iniquity of us all" (Isaiah 53:3–6).

Jesus was *alone.* He had come to His own, and His own received Him not. "But all this was done, that the Scriptures of the prophets might be fulfilled. Then all the disciples forsook him, and fled" (Matthew 26:56). The crowds who had so recently shouted, "Hosanna," had that very day shouted, "Crucify him. Crucify him." Now even His loyal twelve had left. And at last we hear Him cry out, "My God, my God, why hast thou forsaken me?" (Mark 15:34). Not only had He been forsaken by His human companions, but now in that desperate and lonely hour He—because He was bearing our sins in His own body on the cross—had been forsaken by God as well. Jesus was enduring the suffering and judgment of hell for you and me.

Hell, essentially, is separation from God. Hell is the loneliest place in the universe. Jesus suffered its agony for you, in your place. Now God says, Repent, believe on Christ, receive Christ, and you will never know the sorrow, the loneliness, and the agony of hell.

"Whosoever shall call upon the name of the Lord shall be saved" (Romans 10:13).

7

After Death—What?

There is but a step between me and death.
1 Samuel 20:3

IT HAS been said that all of life is but a preparation for death. The psalmist said: "What man is he that liveth, and shall not see death?" (Psalm 89:48).

This is supposed to be a free-thinking age of radical experiment. We have sought to change the world and the laws which govern it through knowledge, science, invention, discovery, philosophy, and materialistic thinking. We have tried to enthrone the false gods of money, fame, and human intelligence; but however we try, the end is always the same: "It is appointed unto men once to die" (Hebrews 9:27).

In the midst of life, we see death on every hand. The wail of the ambulance, the illuminated mortuary signs, the graveyards we so frequently pass, and the sight of a hearse threading its way through traffic all remind us that the Grim Reaper may call for us at any moment. None of us can be sure when that exact moment will be, but we are well aware that it may come at any time.

Someone has said, "The only certain thing about life is death." Oscar Wilde said, "One can survive everything nowadays—except death!" Books on death and dying have proliferated in recent days—as have books by those who claim to have experienced death and come back to tell about it. Rather than looking for a way to make our peace with God, the world has instead come up with classes on dying and how to face death—accepting it as a normal part of living. Actually, all mankind is sitting on Death Row. How we die or when is not the main issue, but where do we go after death.

Each year hundreds of Americans step into their automobiles little realizing this is to be their last ride. In 1980 53,200 Americans died in automobile accidents. In spite of all the increased safety measures, another 469,000 persons were killed in accidents at home, when all thought of death was far from their minds. For death stalks mankind relentlessly, and although medical science and safety engineers wage a constant war against it, in the end, death is always the victor.

Because of this long-fought scientific battle, we now have the advantage of a few years more of life, but death is still standing at the end of the road, and the life span of the average person does not far exceed the biblical three score years and ten.

Heart diseases still cut down far too many of our citizens in the prime of life. Cancer still presses its pain into the bodies of thousands. Blood disorders take their toll, although medical research has greatly decreased their annual number. Herpes and AIDS (acquired immune deficiency syndrome) are the illnesses of the '80s. They are on the rise around the world and have been reported on all the major continents. But however optimistic the statistical surveys, however much our life span has been increased since 1900, whatever the figures may show on murder, suicide, and other forms of violent death, the inevitable fact of death remains unchanged—it is still our ultimate experience on earth!

A Lifelong Battle

From the moment a child is born, the death process, and the fight against it, begins. The mother devotes years of attention to protecting the life of her child. She watches the food, the clothes, the environment, the medical checkups and inoculations, but in spite of her loving care, the child has already begun to die.

Before many years the tangible signs of weakness will be obvious. The dentist will check the decay of our teeth. Glasses will be needed to help improve our fading vision. Skin will wrinkle and sag as time passes, and our shoulders will droop and our step become slower and less sure. The brittleness of our bones will increase as our energy lessens. Almost without realizing it we have begun to move closer to death.

Health insurance and hospitalization will be used to help us cushion the blow. Life insurance will be purchased to cover our final expenses and obligations, and we shall suddenly see our whole life as a great and never-ending battle with death. We shall see that we are all running a race in which the most we can hope for is a little more time, and outwit our opponent as we may, in the end we know that death will always win!

What a mysterious thing is this enemy of ours—as

mysterious as life itself. For the life that we see so plentifully around us in plants and animals, as well as in human beings, cannot be reproduced by us, or even explained. Death is also without explanation, although we are as aware of its presence as we are of life. How little we like to talk about it, however, or consider its importance! When life comes, and a child is born, we rejoice. When life goes, and a man dies, we try to dismiss the thought as quickly as possible.

Today there are something like three billion people living on this planet. Almost all of them will be dead in a hundred years. Their bodies will be without feeling. But what about their souls—the essential and eternal part of life? Here is the mystery. What is missing when a man dies? Where does that missing thing go?

Why Do Men Reject God?

Some years ago a newspaper columnist died in Denver, Colorado. The mourners listened to his recorded voice at the funeral when he said, "This is my funeral. I am an atheist and have been for many years. I have the utmost contempt for theological nonsense. Clergymen are moral cowards. Miracles are the product of the imagination. If any four reporters were sent to an execution and got their facts as twisted as the apostles in the Bible report, they would be fired forthwith. I want no religious songs. This is going to be a perfectly rational funeral."

Contrast this to the beautiful description of death pictured by Alfred Lord Tennyson in his poem *In Memoriam*. "God's finger touched him, and he slept."

Every age has produced men who in their hatred of God have attempted to heap ridicule and abuse upon the church, the Scriptures, and Jesus Christ. Without presenting evidence they cry out against the voice of God. History testifies of the George Bernard Shaws, the Robert Ingersolls, the B. F. Skinners, and many other philosophers who strove, by argument, to destroy the fear of death.

Listen to the anthropologist tell of death in the jungle. There is no "theological nonsense" there, for they have not heard of Jesus Christ. What of death there? In some tribes the old are turned into the bush so that the wild animals might attack them and death need not be faced by the young. In another tribe the clothes are stripped off and the bodies of the mourners painted with white. Hour after hour the moans and screams of the women tell the world that a soul is about to leave a body. Death outside of Christian influence is filled with horror and despair—or, at best, resignation and indifference. Among the Moslems, for instance, death is looked forward to in anticipation, for Moslems believe that great pleasures await the faithful—if they die while killing infidels or fighting for their faith.

Compare this to the death of the Christian. When Christ came He gave a new approach to death. Man had always looked upon death as an enemy, but Jesus said that He had conquered death and taken the very sting out of death. Jesus Christ was the Master Realist when He urged men to prepare for death, which was certain to come. Do not worry, said the Lord Jesus, about the death of the body, but rather concern yourself with the eternal death of the soul.

I think of Helen Morken who, as she lay dying, was surrounded by her husband and children singing hymns for hours each day. Literally, she was sung into the presence of the Lord. And I think of those saints of God described by

Alexander Smellie in his book, *Men of the Covenant*. He tells of the great men of faith who died during those "killing times" in Scotland when executions were anything but pleasant. There were no electric chairs, firing squads, or lethal injections to make death as painless as possible. It was a time of torture—thumb screws, the boot, of being hanged and then quartered. For this reason, each man described by Smellie had a horror of death. Yet, each one, when he came to the actual point of dying, died in an ectasy of joy!

The Bible indicates that there are actually two deaths: one is *physical death* and the other is *eternal death*. Jesus warned that we are to fear the *second death* far more than the *first death*. He described the *second death* as hell, which is eternal separation from God. He indicated that the death of your body is nothing compared to the conscious everlasting banishment of a soul from God.

The Death of a Saint

The last statements of dying men provide an excellent study for those who are looking for realism in the face of death.

Matthew Henry—"Sin is bitter. I bless God I have inward supports."

Martin Luther—"Our God is the God from whom cometh salvation: God is the Lord by whom we escape death."

John Knox—"Live in Christ, live in Christ, and the flesh need not fear death."

John Wesley—"The best of all is, God is with us. Farewell! Farewell!"

Richard Baxter—"I have pain; but I have peace. I have peace."

William Carey, the missionary—"When I am gone, speak less of Dr. Carey and more of Dr. Carey's Savior."

Adoniram Judson—"I am not tired of my work, neither am I tired of the world; yet when Christ calls me home, I shall go with the gladness of a boy bounding away from school."

How different is the story of the Christian who has confessed his sin and by faith received Jesus Christ as his personal Savior!

For many years Dr. Effie Jane Wheeler taught English and literature where I attended college. Dr. Wheeler was noted for her piety as well as for her knowledge of the subjects she taught. In May of 1949, on Memorial Day, Dr. Wheeler wrote the following letter to Dr. Edman, then president of the college, her colleagues, and former students.

"I greatly appreciate the moment in chapel that may be given to reading this, for before you leave for the summer I should like to have you know the truth about me as I learned it myself only last Friday. My doctor at last has given what has been his real diagnosis of my illness for weeks—an inoperable case of cancer. Now if he had been a Christian he wouldn't have been so dilatory or shaken, for he would have known, as you and I do, that life or death is equally welcome when we live in the will and presence of the Lord. If the Lord has chosen me to go to Him soon, I go gladly. Please do not give a moment's grief for me. I do not say a cold goodbye but rather a warm *Auf Wiedersehen* till I see you again—in the blessed land where I may be allowed to draw aside a curtain when you enter. With a heart full of love for every individual of you. (Signed) Effie Jane Wheeler."

Just two weeks after writing this letter, Dr. Wheeler entered the presence of her Savior, who had kept His promise to take the sting out of death.

While we were writing this chapter, in one mail we received four letters. One was from a ninety-four-year-old saint, eager to be with her Lord; one from a woman on Death Row who, since becoming a Christian six years ago, can now look beyond her approaching execution to the glory that lies ahead; and two letters from women whose husbands had just died after many years of marriage (one just short of their forty-ninth wedding anniversary). Each is looking beyond death to the glory that lies ahead.

The great Dwight L. Moody on his deathbed said: "This is my triumph; this is my coronation day! It is glorious!"

The Bible teaches that you are an immortal soul. Your soul is eternal and will live forever. In other words, the real you—the part of you that thinks, feels, dreams, aspires; the ego, the personality—will never die. The Bible teaches that your soul will live forever in one of two places—heaven or hell. If you are not a Christian and you have never been born again, then the Bible teaches that your soul goes immediately to a place Jesus called Hades, where you will await the judgment of God.

An Unpopular Subject

I am conscious of the fact that the subject of hell is not a very pleasant one. It is very unpopular, controversial, and misunderstood. In my crusades across the country, however, I usually devote one evening to the discussion of this subject. Following my discussion many letters to the editors of newspapers appear for days as people argue the pros and cons, for the Bible has almost as much to say about this subject as any other. In student discussions on many campuses of America I am continually asked the question, "What about hell? Is there fire in hell?" and similar questions. As a minister I must deal with it. I cannot ignore it, even though it makes people uncomfortable and anxious. I grant that it is the hardest of all teachings of Christianity to receive.

There are those who teach that everybody eventually will be saved, that God is a God of love and He will never send anyone to hell. They believe that the words *eternal* or *everlasting* do not actually mean forever. However, the same word which speaks of eternal banishment from God is also used for the eternity of heaven. Someone has said that "fairness demands that we make the joy of the righteous and the punishment of the wicked both qualify, as they are the same Greek word and of the same duration."

There are others who teach that after death those who have refused to receive God's plan of redemption are annihilated; they cease to exist. In searching the Bible from cover to cover I cannot find one shred of evidence to support this view. The Bible teaches that whether we are saved or lost, there is conscious and everlasting existence of the soul and personality.

There are others who teach that after death there is still a possibility of salvation, that God will offer a second chance. If this is true, the Bible gives no hint of it because the Bible is continually warning that "now is the accepted time; behold, now is the day of salvation" (2 Corinthians 6:2).

What the Bible Says

Scores of passages of Scripture could be quoted to support the fact that the Bible does teach there is hell for every man who willingly and knowingly rejects Christ as Lord and Savior:

"I am tormented in this flame" (Luke 16:24).

"Whosoever shall say, Thou fool, shall be in danger of hell fire" (Matthew 5:22).

"The Son of Man shall send forth his angels, and they shall gather out of his kingdom all things that offend, and them which do iniquity; and shall cast them into a furnace of fire: there shall be wailing and gnashing of teeth" (Matthew 13:41–42).

"So shall it be at the end of the world: the angels shall come forth, and sever the wicked from among the just, and shall cast them into the furnace of fire: there shall be wailing and gnashing of teeth" (Matthew 13:49–50).

"Then shall he say also unto them on the left hand, Depart from me, ye cursed, into everlasting fire, prepared for the devil and his angels" (Matthew 25:41).

"But he will burn up the chaff with unquenchable fire" (Matthew 3:12).

"In flaming fire taking vengeance on them that know not God, and that obey not the gospel of our Lord Jesus Christ: Who shall be punished with everlasting destruction from the presence of the Lord, and from the glory of his power" (1 Thessalonians 1:8–9).

"The same shall drink of the wine of the wrath of God, which is poured out without mixture into the cup of his indignation; and he shall be tormented with fire and brimstone in the presence of the holy angels, and in the presence of the Lamb: and the smoke of their torment ascendeth up for ever and ever: and they have no rest day nor night" (Revelation 14:10–11).

"And death and hell were cast into the lake of fire. This

is the second death. And whosoever was not found written in the Book of Life was cast into the lake of fire" (Revelation 20:14–15).

"But the fearful, and unbelieving, and the abominable, and murderers, and whoremongers, and sorcerers, and idolaters, and all liars, shall have their part in the lake which burneth with fire and brimstone: which is the second death" (Revelation 21:8).

But I hear someone say, "I don't believe in hell. My religion is the Sermon on the Mount."

Well, let's listen to a passage from the Sermon on the Mount: "And if thy right eye offend thee, pluck it out, and cast it from thee: for it is profitable for thee that one of thy members should perish, and not that thy whole body should be cast into hell. And if thy right hand offend thee, cut it off, and cast it from thee: for it is profitable for thee that one of thy members should perish, and not that thy whole body should be cast into hell" (Matthew 5:29–30).

Here we have the distinct teaching of Jesus that there is a hell. In fact, Jesus told stories and gave illustrations on the subject and warned men time after time about the folly of living a sinful and hypocritical life here on earth.

Hell on Earth

There is no doubt that wicked men suffer a certain hell here on earth. The Bible says, "Be sure your sin will find you out" (Numbers 32:23). Again the Bible says, "Whatsoever a man soweth, that shall he also reap" (Galatians 6:7). However, there is evidence all around us to show that some wicked men seem to prosper and the righteous suffer for their righteousness. The Bible teaches that there is going to be a time of equalization when justice shall be done. Someone has said that "we are not punished for our sins but by them." Both are true.

Will a loving God send a man to hell? The answer is—yes, because He is just. But He does not send him willingly. Man condemns himself by his refusal of God's way of salvation. In love and mercy, God is offering to men and women a way of escape, a way of salvation, a hope and anticipation of better things. Man in his blindness, stupidity, stubbornness, egotism, and love of sinful pleasure refuses God's simple method of escaping the pangs of eternal banishment.

Suppose I am sick and call a doctor, who comes and gives me a prescription. But after thinking it over I decide to ignore his advice and to refuse the medicine. When he returns a few days later he might find my condition much worse. Could I blame the doctor, could I hold him responsible? He gave me the prescription. He prescribed the remedy. But I refused it!

Just so, God prescribes the remedy for the ills of the human race. That remedy is personal faith and commitment to Jesus Christ. The remedy is to be born again, as we will discuss in another chapter. If we deliberately refuse it, then we must suffer the consequence; and we cannot blame God. Is it God's fault because we refuse the remedy?

The man who refuses to believe in life after death, in heaven to gain or hell to shun, the man who refuses to believe what God says in His Word about heaven and hell awakes in the next life to find that he has been wrong, he has lost everything. In *People* magazine, one of the nation's leading gamblers, Lem Banker, has been quoted as saying, "Never bet what you want to win, only what you can afford to lose." Can you afford to lose your eternal soul?

There are others who ask, "What is the nature of hell?" There are four words that have been translated in our Bible as "hell." One word is *Sheol,* which is translated thirty-one times as "hell" in the Old Testament. It means an "unseen state." The words of *sorrow, pain,* and *destruction* are used in connection with it.

The second word is *Hades,* which is translated from the Greek and used ten times in the New Testament. It means the same as *Sheol* in the Old Testament. Judgment and suffering are always connected with it.

The third word is *Tartarus,* used only once in 2 Peter 2:4, where it says that disobedient angels are cast into Tartarus. It indicates a place of judgment, such as a prison, or dungeon, where there is intense darkness.

The fourth word is *Gehenna,* used eleven times and translated as "hell" in the New Testament. It is the illustration that Jesus used of the Valley of Hinnon, a place outside Jerusalem where rubbish and debris were burned continually.

Others ask, "Does the Bible teach literal fire in hell?" If it is not literal fire, it is something worse. Jesus would not have exaggerated. There is no doubt that the Bible many times uses the word *fire* figuratively. However, God does have a fire that burns and yet does not consume.

When Moses saw the bush of fire, he was amazed to find that the bush was not consumed. The three Hebrew children were put in a fiery furnace, but they were not consumed; in fact, not a hair of their heads was singed.

On the other hand, the Bible talks about our tongues being "set on fire of hell" (James 3:6) every time we speak evil about our neighbors. That does not mean that literal combustion takes place every time we say something against our neighbors. But whether it be literal or figurative does not affect its reality. If there is no fire, then God is using symbolic language to indicate something that could be far worse.

Separation from God

Essentially, hell is separation from God. It is the second death, which is described as the eternal conscious banishment from the presence of all that is light, joyous, good, righteous, and happy. The Bible has many fearful descriptions concerning this awful condition in which the soul will find itself one minute after death.

It is strange that men will prepare for everything except death. We prepare for education. We prepare for business. We prepare for our careers. We prepare for marriage. We prepare for old age. We prepare for everything except the moment we are to die. And yet the Bible says it is appointed unto all of us once to die.

Death is an occurrence that to each man seems unnatural when related to himself, but natural when related to others. Death reduces all men to the same rank. It strips the rich of his millions and the poor man of his rags. It cools avarice and stills the fires of passion. All would like to ignore death, and yet all must face it—the prince and the peasant, the fool and the philosopher, the murderer and the saint alike. Death knows no age limits, no partiality. It is a thing that all men fear.

Toward the end of his life, Daniel Webster related how once he attended a church service in a quiet country village. The clergyman was a simple-hearted, pious old man.

After the opening exercises he arose and pronounced his text, and then with the utmost simplicity and earnestness said, "My friends, we can die but once."

Daniel Webster, commenting on this sermon, later said, "Frigid and weak as these words might seem, at once they were to me among the most impressive and awakening I ever heard."

An Appointment with Death

It is easy to think of others having to keep this appointment with death, but difficult for us to remember that we, too, must keep this same appointment. When we see soldiers going to the front or read of a condemned prisoner or visit a dying friend, we are conscious of a certain solemnity which gathers about such persons. Death is appointed for all, and the question of its occurrence is merely a matter of time. Other appointments in life—the appointment of pleasure—we can neglect or break and take the consequence, but here is an appointment that no man can ignore, no man can break. He can meet it only *once* but meet it he must!

If physical death were the only consequence of a life lived apart from God, we would not have so much to fear, but the Bible warns that there is the second death, which is the eternal banishment from God.

However, there is a brighter side. As the Bible pronounces hell for the sinner, it also promises heaven for the saint. A saint has been described as a sinner who has been forgiven. The subject of heaven is much easier to accept than the subject of hell. And yet the Bible teaches both.

If you are moving to a new home, you want to know all about the community to which you are going. If you are transferring to another city, you want to know all about the city—its railroads, industries, parks, lakes, schools, etc. And since we are going to spend eternity someplace, we ought to know something about it. The information concerning heaven is found in the Bible. It is right that we should think about it and talk about it. In talking about heaven, earth grows shabby by comparison. Our sorrows and problems here seem so much less when we have keen anticipation of the future. In a certain sense the Christian has heaven here on earth. He has peace of soul, peace of conscience, and peace with God. In the midst of troubles and difficulties he has an inner peace and joy, not dependent on circumstances.

There Is a Heaven

But the Bible also promises the Christian a heaven in the life hereafter. Someone asked John Quincy Adams at the age of ninety-four how he felt one morning. He said, "Quite well. Quite well. But the house I live in is not so good." Even though the house we live in may be sick and weak, we can actually feel strong and sure if we are Christians. Jesus taught there is a heaven.

There are a number of passages that could be quoted, but the most descriptive is found in John 14:2: "In my Father's house are many rooms; if it were not so, would I have told you that I go to prepare a place for you? And when I go and prepare a place for you, I will come again and receive you to myself, that where I am there you may be also" (RSV). Paul was so certain of heaven that he could say, "We are confident, I say, and willing rather to be absent from the body and to be present with the Lord" (2 Corinthians 5:8).

How different is the anticipation of the Christian and that of the agnostic Bob Ingersoll, who said at the grave of his brother, "Life is a narrow veil between the cold and barren peaks of two eternities. We strive in vain to look beyond the heights. We cry aloud and the only answer is the echo of our wailing cry."

The apostle Paul said time after time, "We know," "We are confident," "We are always confident." The Bible says that Abraham "looked for a city which hath foundations, whose builder and maker is God."

Many people say, "Do you believe that heaven is a literal place?" Yes! Jesus said, "I go to prepare a place for you." The Bible teaches that Enoch and Elijah ascended in a literal body to a literal place that is just as real as Hawaii, Switzerland, the Virgin Islands, or more so!

Many people have asked, "Where is heaven?" We are not told in the Scripture where heaven is. Nor does it matter. It will be heaven and Christ will be there to welcome us home.

A Place of Beauty

The Bible teaches that this country will be a place of beauty. It is described in the Bible as "a building of God"—"a city"—"a better country"—"an inheritance"—"a glory."

You may ask, "Will we know each other in heaven?" The Bible indicates in a number of places that it will be a time of grand reunion with those who have gone on before.

Others say, "Do you believe that children will be saved?" Yes. The Bible indicates that God does not hold a child accountable for his or her sins until he reaches the age of accountability. There seems to be plenty of indication that the atonement covers their sin until they reach an age at which they are responsible for their own right and wrong actions.

The Bible also indicates that heaven will be a place of great understanding and knowledge of things that we never learned down here.

Sir Isaac Newton, when an old man, said to one who praised his wisdom, "I am as a child on the seashore picking up a pebble here and a shell there, but the great ocean of truth still lies before me."

And Thomas Edison once said, "I do not know one millionth part of one percent about anything."

Many of the mysteries of God, the heartaches, trials, disappointments, tragedies, and the silence of God in the midst of suffering will be revealed there. Elie Wiesel said that eternity is ". . . the place where questions and answers become one." And in John 16:23 Jesus says, "And in that day ye shall ask me nothing." All our questions will be answered!

Many people ask, "Well, what will we do in heaven? Just sit down and enjoy the luxuries of life?" No. The Bible indicates that we will serve God. There will be work to do for God. Our very beings will praise God. The Bible says, "And there shall be no more curse; but the throne of God and of the Lamb shall be in it; and his servants shall serve him" (Revelation 22:3).

It will be a time of total joy, service, laughter, singing, and praise to God. Imagine serving Him forever and never growing tired!

Into the Presence of Christ

Now the Bible teaches to be absent from the body is to be present with the Lord. The moment a Christian dies, he goes immediately into the presence of Christ. There his soul awaits the resurrection, when the soul and body will be rejoined.

Many people ask, "How can the bodies that have decayed or been cremated be raised?" God knows. But the new body that we will have will be a glorious body like the body of Christ. It will be an eternal body. It will never know tears, heartache, tragedy, disease, suffering, death, or fatigue. It will be a renewed body, but still recognizable.

Here we have a picture of two eternal worlds floating out into space. Every son of Adam will be on one or the other. There is a great deal of mystery surrounding both of them, but there are enough hints and implications in the Bible to give us light that one will be a world of tragedy and suffering and the other will be one of light and glory.

We have now seen the problems of the human race. Superficially, they are complex; basically, they are simple. We have seen that they could probably be summed up in one word—sin. We have seen that man's future is hopeless without God. But just to analyze our problems and have an intellectual understanding of God's plan is not enough. If God is to help man, then man must meet certain conditions. In the next few chapters we will survey these conditions.

PART TWO

Advancing the Solution

8

Why Jesus Came

The Son of man is come to seek and to save that which was lost.

Luke 19:10

WE HAVE seen that the most terrible, the most devastating fact in the universe is sin. The cause of all trouble, the root of all sorrow, the dread of every man lies in this one small word—sin. It has crippled the nature of man. It has destroyed the inner harmony of man's life. It has robbed him of his nobility. It has caused man to be caught in the devil's trap.

All mental disorders, all sicknesses, all perversions, all destruction, all wars find their *original* root in sin. It causes madness in the brain and poison in the heart. It is described in the Bible as a fatal disease that demands a radical cure. It is a tornado on the loose. It is a volcano gone wild. It is a madman escaped from the asylum. It is a gangster on the prowl. It is a roaring lion seeking its prey. It is a streak of lightning heading toward the earth. It is quicksand sucking man under. It is a deadly cancer eating its way into the souls of men. It is a raging torrent that sweeps everything before it. It is a cesspool of corruption contaminating every area of life.

But, as someone has said, "Sin can keep you from the Bible—or the Bible can keep you from sin."

For ages men were lost in spiritual darkness, blinded by the disease of sin, made to grope—searching, questing, seeking some way out. Man needed someone who could lead him out of the mental confusion and moral labyrinth, someone who could unlock the prison doors and redeem him from the devil's prison. Men with hungry hearts, thirsty minds, and broken spirits stood hopelessly with searching eyes and listening ears. Meanwhile the devil gloated over his mighty victory in the Garden of Eden.

From the primitive man in the jungle through the mighty civilizations of Egypt, Greece, and Rome, bewildered men were all asking the same question, "How can I get out? How can I be better? What can I do? Which way can I turn? How can I get rid of this terrible disease? How can I stop this onrushing torrent? How can I get out of the mess in which I find myself? If there is a way, how can I find it?"

The Bible's Answer

We have already seen how the Bible teaches that God was a God of love. He wanted to do something for man. He wanted to save man. He wanted to free man from the curse of sin. How could He do it? God was a just God. He was righteous and holy. He had warned man from the beginning that if he obeyed the devil and disobeyed God, he would die physically and spiritually. Man deliberately disobeyed God. Man had to die or God would have been a liar, for God could not break His word. His very nature would not allow Him to lie. His word had to be kept. Therefore, when man deliberately disobeyed Him, he was banished from the presence of God. He deliberately chose to go the devil's way.

There had to be some other way, for man was hopelessly involved and helplessly lost. Man's very nature was inverted. He opposed God. Many even denied that God existed, so blinded were they by the disease from which they suffered.

But even in the Garden of Eden, God gave a hint that He was going to do something about it. He warned the devil and promised man, "And I will put enmity between thee and the woman, and between thy seed and her seed; it shall bruise thy head, and thou shalt bruise his heel" (Genesis 3:15). "And thou shalt bruise his heel"—here was a brilliant flash of light from heaven. The head refers to a total permanent wound; the heel refers to a temporary injury. Here was a promise. Here was something that man could hold on to. God was promising that some day a Redeemer would come, a Deliverer would come. God gave man hope. Down through the centuries man held on to that one bit of hope!

That was not all. There were other occasions through the thousands of years of history when other flashes of light came from heaven. All through the Old Testament, God gave man the promise of salvation if by faith he would believe in the coming Redeemer. Therefore God began to teach His people that man could only be saved by substitution. Someone else would have to pay the penalty for man's redemption.

Go Back to Eden

Go back again with me in your imagination to Eden for a moment. God said, "In the day that thou eatest thereof thou shalt surely die." Man did eat of it. He died.

Suppose that God had said, "Adam, you must have made a mistake, that was a slight error on your part. You are forgiven. Please don't do it again." God would have been a liar. He would not have been holy, neither would He have been just. He was forced by His very nature to keep His word. God's justice was at stake. Man had to die spiritually and physically. His iniquities had separated him from his God. Thus man had to suffer. He had to pay for his own sins. As we have seen, Adam was the federal head of the human race. When Adam sinned, we all sinned. "Wherefore, as by one man sin entered into the world, and death by sin; and so death passed upon all men, for that all have sinned" (Romans 5:12).

The burning question became "How can God be just and still justify the sinner?" It must be remembered that the word justify means the "clearance of the soul from guilt." Justification is far more than just forgiveness. Sin must be put away and made as though it had never been. Man must be restored so that there shall be no spot or blemish or stain. In other words, man must be taken back to the position he had before he fell from grace.

For centuries men in their blindness have been trying to get back to Eden—but they have never been able to reach their goal. They have tried many paths, but they have all failed. C. S. Lewis says that "All religions are either a preview or a perversion of Christianity."

Education is important, but education will not bring a man back to God. False religions are an opiate which attempt to keep men from present misery while promising future glory, but they will never bring man to the place of his goal. The United Nations may be a practical necessity in a world of men at war, and we are thankful for every step that can be taken in the field of international relations to settle disputes without recourse to war; but if the United Nations could bring lasting peace, man could say to God, "We do not need You any more. We have brought peace on earth and have organized humanity in righteousness." All of these schemes are patchwork remedies that a sick and dying world must use while waiting for the Great Physician. Back in history we know that the first attempt of united man ended with the confusion of tongues at the Tower of Babel. Men have failed on every other occasion when they have tried to work without God, and they will continue to be doomed to such failures.

The question remains "How can God be just—that is, true to Himself in nature and true to Himself in holiness—and yet justify the sinner?" Because each man had to bear his own sins, all mankind was excluded from helping, since each was contaminated with the same disease.

The only solution was for an innocent party to volunteer to die physically and spiritually as a substitution before God. This innocent party would have to take man's judgment, penalty, and death. But where was such an individual? Certainly there was none perfect on earth, for the Bible says, "All have sinned" (Romans 3:23). There was only one possibility. God's own Son was the only personality in the universe who had the capacity to bear in His own body the sins of the whole world. Certainly Gabriel or Michael the archangel might possibly have come and died for one, but only God's Son was infinite and thus able to die for all.

God in Three Persons

The Bible teaches that God is actually three Persons. This is a mystery that we will never be able to understand. The Bible does not teach that there are three Gods—but that there is one God. This one God, however, is expressed in three Persons. There is God the Father, God the Son, and God the Holy Spirit.

The Second Person of this Trinity is God's Son, Jesus Christ. He is co-equal with God the Father. He was not *a* Son of God but *the* Son of God. He is the Eternal Son of God—the Second Person of the Holy Trinity, God manifested in the flesh, the living Savior.

The Bible teaches that Jesus Christ had no beginning. He was never created. The Bible teaches that the heavens were created by Him (John 1:1–3). All the myriads of stars and flaming suns were created by Him. The earth was flung from His flaming fingertip. The birth of Jesus Christ that we celebrate at Christmas time was not His beginning. His origin is shrouded in that same mystery that baffles us when we inquire into the beginning of God. The Bible only tells us, "In the beginning was the Word, and the Word was with God, and the Word was God" (John 1:1).

About Christ, the Bible teaches us, "Who is the image of the invisible God, the firstborn of every creature: For by him were all things created, that are in heaven, and that are in earth, visible and invisible, whether they be thrones, or dominions, or principalities, or powers: all things were created by him, and for him: And he is before all things, and by him all things consist" (Colossians 1:15–17).

That last phrase indicates that He holds all things together. In other words, the entire universe would smash into billions of atoms were it not for the cohesive power of

Jesus Christ. The Bible again says, "And, thou, Lord, in the beginning has laid the foundation of the earth; and the heavens are the works of thine hands: They shall perish; but thou remainest; and they all shall wax old as doth a garment; And as a vesture shalt thou fold them up, and they shall be changed: but thou art the same, and thy years shall not fail" (Hebrews 1:10–12).

Jesus Christ, the Redeemer

Again Jesus said of Himself, "I am Alpha and Omega, the beginning and the end." He, and He alone, had the power and capacity to bring man back to God. But would He? If He did, He would have to come to earth. He would have to take the form of a servant. He would have to be made in the likeness of men. He would have to humble Himself and become obedient unto death. He would have to grapple with sin. He would have to meet and overcome Satan, the enemy of man's souls. He would have to redeem sinners out of the slave market of sin. He would have to loose the bonds and set the prisoners free by paying a price—that price would be His own life. He would have to be despised and rejected of men, a man of sorrows and acquainted with grief. He would have to be smitten of God and separated from God. He would have to be wounded for the transgressions of men and bruised for their iniquities, His blood shed to atone for man's sin. He would have to reconcile God and man. He would be the great Mediator of history. He would have to be a substitute. He would have to die in the place of sinful man. All this would have to be done—voluntarily.

And that is exactly what happened! Looking down over

the battlements of heaven He saw this planet swinging in space—doomed, damned, crushed, and bound for hell. He saw you and me struggling beneath our load of sin and bound in the chains and ropes of sin. He made His decision in the council halls of God. The angelic hosts bowed in humility and awe as heaven's Prince of Princes and Lord of Lords, who could speak worlds into space, got into His jeweled chariot, went through pearly gates and across the steep of the skies, and on a black Judean night, while the stars sang together and the escorting angels chanted His praises, stepped out of the chariot, threw off His robes, and became man!

It was as though I, while walking along a road, stepped on an ant hill. I might look down and say to the ants, "I am terribly sorry that I've stepped on your ant hill. I've disrupted your home. Everything is in confusion. I wish I could tell you that I care, that I did not mean to do it, that I would like to help you."

But you say, "That's absurd, that's impossible, ants cannot understand your language!" That's just it! How wonderful it would be if I could only become an ant for a few moments and in their own language tell them of my concern for them!

That, in effect, is what Christ did. He came to reveal God to men. He it is who told us that God loves us and is interested in our lives. He it is who told us of the mercy and long-suffering and grace of God. He it is who promised life everlasting.

But more than that, Jesus Christ partook of flesh and blood in order that He might die (Hebrews 2:14). "He was manifested to take away our sins" (1 John 3:5). The very purpose of Christ's coming into the world was that He might offer up His life as a sacrifice for the sins of men. He came to die. The shadow of His death hung like a pall over all of His thirty-three years.

The night Jesus was born Satan trembled. He sought to slay Him before He was born and tried to slay Him as soon as He was born. When the decree went forth from Herod ordering the slaughter of all the children, its one purpose was to make certain of the death of Jesus.

The Sinless Son

All the days of His life on earth He never once committed a sin. He is the only man who ever lived who was sinless. He could stand in front of men and ask, "Which of you convinceth me of sin?" (John 8:46). He was hounded by the enemy day and night, but they never found any sin in Him. He was without spot or blemish.

Jesus lived a humble life. He made Himself of no reputation. He received no honor of men. He was born in a stable. He was reared in the insignificant village of Nazareth. He was a carpenter. He gathered around Him a humble group of fishermen as His followers. He walked among men as a man. He was one of the people. He humbled Himself as no other man has ever humbled himself.

Jesus taught with such authority that the people of His day said, "Never man spake like this man" (John 7:46). Every word that He spoke was historically true. Every word that He spoke was scientifically true. Every word that He spoke was ethically true. There were no loopholes in the moral conceptions and statements of Jesus Christ. His ethical vision was wholly correct, correct in the age in which He lived and correct in every age that has followed it.

The words of this blessed Person were prophetically true. He prophesied many things that are even yet in the future. Lawyers tried to catch Him with test questions, but they could never confuse Him. His answers to His opponents were clear and cleancut. There were no question marks about His statements, no deception in His meaning, no hesitancy in His words. He knew, and therefore spoke with quiet authority. He spoke with such simplicity that the common people heard Him gladly. Though His words were profound, they were plain. His words were weighty, yet they shone with a luster and simplicity of statement that staggered His enemies. He dealt with the great questions of the day in such a way that, from simple to sophisticated, man had no difficulty in understanding Him.

The Lord Jesus cured the sick, the lame, the halt, and the blind. He healed the leper and raised the dead. He cast out demons. He quieted the elements. He stilled storms. He brought peace, joy, and hope to the thousands to whom He ministered.

He showed no sign of fear. He was never in a hurry. He met with no accidents. He moved with perfect coordination and precision. He had supreme poise of bearing. He did not waver or worry about His work. Though He did not heal all the sick, raise all the dead, open the eyes of all the blind, or feed all the hungry, yet at the end of His life He could say, "I have finished the work thou gavest me to do."

He stood before Pilate and quietly said, "Thou couldst have no power at all against me, except it were given thee from above" (John 19:11). He told the frightened people that angelic legions were at His command.

He approached His cross with dignity and calmness, with an assurance and a set purpose that fulfilled the prophecy written about Him eight hundred years earlier: "He is brought as a lamb to the slaughter, and as a sheep before her shearers is dumb, so he openeth not his mouth" (Isaiah 53:7).

Defeating the Devil

He moved supremely, gloriously, and with great anticipation toward the mission that He had come to accomplish. He had come to save sinful men. He had come to appease the wrath of God. He had come to defeat the devil forever. He had come to conquer hell and the grave. There was only one way that He could do it. There was only one course set before Him.

His death had been prophesied thousands of years before. First, as we have seen, in Eden's Garden; and then in sermon, story and prophecy the death of Christ was set forth in the ages past. Abraham foresaw His death as the lamb was slain. The children of Israel symbolized His death in the slaughtered lamb. Every time blood was shed on a Jewish altar it represented the Lamb of God who was someday to come and take away sin. David prophesied His death in detail in more than one prophetic psalm. Isaiah devoted whole chapters to predicting the details of His death.

Jesus Christ said that He had power to lay down His life when He said, "The good shepherd giveth his life for the sheep" (John 10:11). He said again, "Even so must the Son of man be lifted up: That whosoever believeth in him should not perish" (John 3:14, 15). Jesus Christ had faced the possibility of the cross far back in eternity. During all the ages which preceded His birth, He knew that the day of His death was hastening on. When He was born of a virgin, He was born with the cross darkening His pathway. He had taken on a human body in order that He might die. From the cradle to the cross, His purpose was to die.

Someone has described how He suffered as no man has ever suffered: "The night watches in Gethsemane, lighted by the flaming torches, the kiss of the traitor, the arrest, the trial before the high priest, the hour of waiting, the palace of the Roman governor, the journey to the palace of Herod, the rough handling by Herod's brutal soldiers, the awesome scenes while Pilate tried to save Him as priests and people clamored for His blood, the scourging, the howling multitudes, the path from Jerusalem to Golgotha, the nails in His hands, the spike through His feet, the crown of thorns upon His brow, the sarcastic and mocking cries of the two thieves on either side, 'You have saved others, now save yourself.'"

Sometimes people have asked me why Christ died so quickly, in six hours, on the cross, while other victims agonized on the cross for two and three days—and longer. He was weak and exhausted when He came there. He had been scourged, He was physically depleted. But when Christ died, He died voluntarily. He chose the exact moment when He expired.

There He hung between heaven and earth. Having suffered unspeakably, He voiced neither complaint nor appeal but simply a statement by which He let us know in two words something of the terrible physical pain He suffered when he said, "I thirst."

Some unknown poet has put it this way:

But more than pains wracked Him there
Was the deep longing thirst divine

That thirsted for the souls of men,
Dear Lord—and one was mine!

Sinner or Substitute

God demands death, either for the sinner or a substitute. Christ was the substitute! Gabriel and ten legions of angels hovered on the rim of the universe, their swords unsheathed. One look from His blessed face and they would have swept the angry, shouting multitudes into hell. The spikes never held Him—it was the cords of love that bound tighter than any nails that men could mold. "But God commendeth his love toward us, in that, while we were yet sinners, Christ died for us" (Romans 5:8).

For you! For me! He bore our sins in His body upon the tree. As someone has said, "Behold Him on the Cross, bending His sacred head, and gathering into His heart in the awful isolation of separation from God the issue of the sin of the world, and see how out of that acceptance of the issue of sin He creates that which He does not require for Himself that He may distribute to those whose place He has taken." Standing overwhelmed in the presence of this suffering, feeling our own inability to understand or explain, and with a great sense of might and majesty overwhelming us, we hear the next words that pass His lips, "It is finished."

But the physical suffering of Jesus Christ was not the real suffering. Many men before Him had died. Others had hung on a cross longer than He did. Many men had become martyrs. The awful suffering of Jesus Christ was His spiritual death. He reached the final issue of sin, fathomed the deepest sorrow, when He cried, "My God, why hast thou forsaken me?" This cry was proof that Christ, becoming sin for us, had died physically, and with it He lost all sense of the Father's presence at that moment in time. Alone in the supreme hour of mankind's history Christ uttered these words! Light blazed forth to give us a glimpse of what He was enduring, but the light was so blinding, as G. Campbell Morgan says, "that no eye could bear to gaze." The words were uttered, as Dr. Morgan has so well expressed it, "that we men may know how much there is that may not be known."

He who knew no sin was made to be sin on our behalf that we might become the righteousness of God in Him (Galatians 3:13; Mark 15:34; 2 Corinthians 5:21). On the cross He was made sin. He was God-forsaken. Because He knew no sin there is a value beyond comprehension in the penalty He bore, a penalty that He did not need for Himself. If in bearing sin in His own body He created a value that He did not need for Himself, for whom was the value created?

How it was accomplished in the depth of the darkness man will never know. I know only one thing—He bore my sins in His body upon the tree. He hung where I should have hung. The pains of hell that were my portion were heaped on Him, and I am able to go to heaven and merit that which is not my own, but is His by every right. All the types, the offerings, the shadows, and the symbols of the Old Testament were now fulfilled. No longer do the priests have to enter once a year into the Holiest Place. The sacrifice was complete.

Now that the ground of redemption has been laid, all the guilty sinner has to do is believe on the Son, and he can have peace with God. "For God so loved the world, that he gave his only begotten Son, that whosoever believeth in him should not perish, but have everlasting life" (John 3:16).

Three Things in the Cross

In the cross of Christ I see three things: First, a description of the depth of *man's sin*. Do not blame the people of that day for hanging Christ on the cross. You and I are just as guilty. It was not the people or the Roman soldiers who put Him to the cross—it was your sins and my sins that made it necessary for Him to volunteer this death.

Second, in the cross I see the overwhelming *love of God*. If ever you should doubt the love of God, take a long, deep look at the cross, for in the cross you find the expression of God's love.

Third, in the cross is the only *way of salvation*. Jesus said, "I am the way, the truth and the life: no man cometh unto the Father but by me" (John 14:6). There is no possibility of being saved from sin and hell except by identifying yourself with the Christ of the cross. If there had been any other way to save you, He would have found it. If reformation, or living a good moral and ethical life would have saved you, Jesus never would have died. A substitute had to take your place. Men do not like to talk about it. They do not like to hear about it because it injures their pride. It takes all self out.

Many people say, "Can I not be saved by living by the Golden Rule? Or following the precepts of Jesus? Or living the ethical life that Jesus taught?" Even if we could be saved by living the life that Jesus taught, we still would be sinners. We still would fail, because not one of us has ever lived the life that Jesus taught from the time we were born till the time we die. We have failed. We have transgressed. We have disobeyed. We have sinned. Therefore, what are we going to do about that sin? There is only one thing to do and that is to bring it to the cross and find forgiveness.

Years ago King Charles V was loaned a large sum of money by a merchant in Antwerp. The note came due, but the King was bankrupt and unable to pay. The merchant gave a great banquet for the King. When all the guests were seated and before the food was brought in, the merchant had a large platter placed on the table before him and a fire lighted on it. Then, taking the note out of his pocket, he held it in the flames until it was burned to ashes.

Just so, we have all been mortgaged to God. The debt was due, but we were unable to pay. Two thousand years ago God invited a morally corrupt world to the foot of the cross. There God held your sins and mine to the flames until every last vestige of our guilt was consumed.

The Bible says, "Without shedding of blood is no remission" (Hebrews 9:22). Many people have said to me, "How repulsive! You don't mean to tell us that you believe in a slaughterhouse religion!" Others have wondered, "I do not understand why God demands blood." Many people have wondered, "I cannot understand why Christ had to die for me." Today the idea of the shed blood of Christ is becoming old-fashioned and out of date in a lot of preaching. It is in the Bible. It is the very heart of Christianity. The distinctive feature of Christianity is blood atonement. Without it we cannot be saved. Blood is actually a symbol of the death of Christ.

Recently I was standing at the admissions desk at Mayo Clinic in Rochester, Minnesota. There, in a little box, were a number of folders entitled "A Gift of Blood" lettered in red forming a large drop of blood. My first reaction was that this must be a gospel tract, but on looking more closely I saw that it was a challenge to people to assist in the blood program. Blood could mean the difference between life and death for someone ill in the hospital. No one who has ever had to receive a blood transfusion will look upon that blood with anything but gratitude. Some might say that blood taken is somewhat revolting, but blood given is a blessing!

The fact remains that blood represents life, as Leviticus 17:11 says, "For the life of the flesh is in the blood and I have given it for you . . . to make atonement for your soul." So the blood sacrifice runs throughout the Old Testament—a foreshadowing or a symbol of Christ's perfect sacrifice.

Five Things Blood Brings

The Bible teaches that it first of all *redeems*. "Forasmuch as ye know that ye were not redeemed with corruptible things, as silver and gold, from your vain conversation received by tradition from your fathers; But with the precious blood of Christ, as of a lamb without blemish and without spot" (1 Peter 1:18–19). Not only are we redeemed from the hands of the devil, but from the hands of the law handed down by God through Moses. Christ's death on the cross brings me out from under the law. The law condemned me, but Christ satisfied every claim. All the gold and silver and the precious stones of earth could never have bought me. What they could not do, the death of Christ did. Redemption means "buying back." We had been sold for nothing to the devil, but Christ redeemed us and brought us back.

Second, it *brings us nigh.* "But now in Christ Jesus ye who sometimes were far off are made nigh by the blood of Christ" (Ephesians 2:13). When we were "aliens from the commonwealth of Israel, and strangers from the covenants of promise, having no hope, and without God in the world," Jesus Christ brought us nigh unto God. "There is therefore now no condemnation [judgment] to them which are in Christ Jesus" (Romans 8:1). The redeemed sinner will never have to face the judgment of Almighty God. Christ has already taken his judgment.

Third, it *makes peace.* "And, having made peace through the blood of his cross, by him to reconcile all things unto himself; by him, I say, whether they be things in earth, or things in heaven" (Colossians 1:20). The world will never know peace until it finds it in the cross of Jesus Christ. You will never know the peace with God, peace of conscience, peace of mind, and peace of soul until you stand at the foot of the cross and identify yourself with Christ by faith. There is the secret of peace. This is peace with God.

Fourth, it *justifies.* "Much more then, being now justified by his blood, we shall be saved from wrath through him" (Romans 5:9). It changes men's standing before God. It is a change from guilt and condemnation to pardon and forgiveness. The forgiven sinner is not like the discharged prisoner who has served out his term and is discharged but with no further rights of citizenship. The repentant sinner, pardoned through the blood of Jesus Christ, regains his full citizenship. "Who shall lay any thing to the charge of God's elect? It is God that justifieth. Who is he that condemneth? It is Christ that died, yea rather, that is risen again, who is even at the right hand of God, who also maketh intercession for us" (Romans 8:33–34).

Fifth, it *cleanses.* "But if we walk in the light, as he is in the light, we have fellowship one with another, and the blood of Jesus Christ his Son cleanseth us from all sin" (1 John 1:7). The key word in this verse is *all.* Not part of our sins, but *all* of them. Every lie you ever told, every mean, low-down dirty thing that you ever did, your hypocrisy, your lustful thoughts—all are cleansed by the death of Christ.

Just As I Am

The story has often been told that years ago, in London, there was a large gathering of noted people, and among the invited guests was a famous preacher of his day, Caesar Milan. A young lady played and sang charmingly and everyone was delighted. Very graciously, tactfully, and yet boldly the preacher went up to her after the music had ceased and said, "I thought as I listened to you tonight, how tremendously the cause of Christ would be benefited if your talents were dedicated to His cause. You know, young lady, you are as much a sinner in the sight of God as a drunkard in the ditch or a harlot on scarlet street. But I'm glad to tell you that the blood of Jesus Christ, His Son, can cleanse from all sin."

The young woman snapped out a rebuke for his presumption, to which he replied, "Lady, I mean no offense. I pray God's Spirit will convict you."

They all returned to their homes. The young woman retired but could not sleep. The face of the preacher appeared before her and his words rang through her mind. At two o'clock in the morning she sprang from her bed, took a pencil and paper, and with tears streaming down her face, Charlotte Elliott wrote her famous poem:

Just as I am, without one plea,
But that Thy blood was shed for me,
And that Thou bidd'st me come to Thee,
O Lamb of God, I come! I come!
Just as I am, and waiting not
To rid my soul of one dark blot,
To Thee, whose blood can cleanse each spot,
O Lamb of God, I come! I come!

But this is not the end. We do not leave Christ hanging on a cross with blood streaming down from His hands, His side, and His feet. He is taken down and laid carefully away in a tomb. A big stone is rolled against the entrance of the tomb. Soldiers are set to guard it. All day Saturday, His followers sit gloomily and sadly in the upper room. Two have already started toward Emmaus. Fear has gripped them all. Early on that first Easter morning, Mary, Mary Magdalene, and Salome make their way to the tomb to anoint the dead body. When they arrive, they are startled to find the tomb empty. As Alfred Edersheim, the Jewish scholar, writes, "There was no sign of haste, but all was orderly, leaving the impression of One Who had leisurely divested Himself of what no longer befitted Him." An angel is standing at the head of the tomb and asks, "Whom do you seek?" And they reply, "We seek Jesus of Nazareth." And then the angel gives the greatest, most glorious news that human ear has ever heard, "He is not here, He is risen."

The Fact of the Resurrection

Upon that great fact hangs the entire plan of the redemptive program of God. Without the resurrection there could be no salvation. Christ predicted His resurrection many times. He said on one occasion, "For as Jonah was three days and three nights in the whale's belly; so shall the Son of man be three days and three nights in the heart of the earth" (Matthew 12:40). As He predicted, He rose!

There are certain laws of evidence which hold in the establishment of any historic event. There must be documentation of the event in question made by reliable contemporary witnesses. There is more evidence that Jesus rose from the dead than there is that Julius Caesar ever lived or that Alexander the Great died at the age of thirty-three. It is strange that historians will accept thousands of facts for which they can produce only shreds of evidence. But in the face of the overwhelming evidence of the resurrection of Jesus Christ they cast a skeptical eye and hold intellectual doubts. The trouble with these people is that they do not want to believe. Their spiritual vision is so blinded and they are so completely prejudiced that they cannot accept the glorious fact of the resurrection of Christ on Bible testimony alone.

The resurrection meant, first, that Christ was undeniably God. He was what He claimed to be. Christ was Deity in the flesh.

Second, it meant that God had accepted His atoning work on the cross, which was necessary to our salvation. "Who was delivered for our offenses, and was raised again for our justification" (Romans 4:25).

Third, it assures mankind of a righteous judgment. "For as by one man's disobedience many were made sinners, so by the obedience of one shall many be made righteous" (Romans 5:19).

Fourth, it guarantees that our bodies also will be raised

in the end. "But now is Christ risen from the dead, and become the firstfruits of them that slept" (1 Corinthians 15:20). The Scripture teaches that as Christians, our bodies may go to the grave but they are going to be raised on the great resurrection morning. Then will death be swallowed up in victory. As a result of the resurrection of Christ the sting of death is gone and Christ Himself holds the keys. He says, "I am he that liveth, and was dead; and, behold, I am alive forevermore, Amen; and have the keys of hell and death" (Revelation 1:18). And Christ promises that "Because I live, ye shall live also."

And, fifth, it means that death will ultimately be abolished. The power of death has been broken and death's fear has been removed. Now we can say with the Psalmist, "Yea, though I walk through the valley of the shadow of death, I will fear no evil: for thou art with me; Thy rod and thy staff they comfort me" (Psalm 23:4).

Paul looked forward to death with great anticipation as a result of the resurrection of Christ. He said, "For to me to live is Christ, and to die is gain" (Philippians 1:21). As Velma Barfield on Death Row in North Carolina said: "I love Him so much I can hardly wait to see Him."

Without the resurrection of Christ there could be no hope for the future. The Bible promises that someday we are going to stand face to face with the resurrected Christ, and we are going to have bodies like unto His own body.

Face to face with Christ my Savior,
Face to face, what will it be?
When with rapture I behold Him,

Jesus Christ who died for me?
Face to face I shall behold Him,
Far beyond the starry sky;
Face to face in all His glory
I shall see Him by and by.

Carrie E. Breck

9

How and Where to Begin

Except ye be converted, and become as little children, ye shall not enter into the kingdom of heaven.

Matthew 18:3

WE NOW recognize that there is a natural principle which pulls us down to the animal plane—blinding reason, searing conscience, paralyzing will. It is the pull of spiritual gravity. We stand condemned by our own deeds.

God is a holy and righteous God. He cannot tolerate sin. Sin separates from God. It brings the wrath of God upon the human soul. Man has lost his moral, intellectual, and spiritual sense of God because he has lost God. He will not find God until he finds the way back to God.

The way back to God is not an intellectual way. It is not a moral way. You cannot *think* your way back to God because human thought-life will not coordinate with divine thought-life, for the carnal mind is at enmity with God. You cannot *worship* your way back to God because man is a spiritual rebel from God's presence. You cannot *moralize* your way back to God because character is flawed with sin.

The Way Back to God

The natural questions come to you—What shall I do? Where shall I start? Where do I begin? What is my road back to God? There is only *one way* back to God. Jesus said, "Except ye be converted, and become as little children, ye shall not enter into the kingdom of heaven" (Matthew 18:3). It is significant that Jesus did not tell the little children to become as His disciples, but His disciples to become as little children. By childlike faith, *everyone* has a chance, from feeble-minded to intellectuals. Thus Jesus demanded a conversion. This is how to begin! This is where it starts! You must be converted!

There are many people who confuse conversion with the keeping of the law. The law of Moses is set forth in specific terms in the Bible and the purpose of the law is made very clear. It was not offered at any time as a panacea for the world's ills. Rather, it was given as a diagnosis of the world's ills; it outlines the reason for our trouble, not the cure. The Bible says, "Now we know that what things soever the law saith, it saith to them who are under the law: that every mouth may be stopped, and all the world may become guilty before God" (Romans 3:19). The law has given a revelation of man's unrighteousness, and the Bible says, "By the deeds of the law there shall no flesh be justified in his sight" (Romans 3:20). It is impossible to be converted by the keeping of the law. The Bible says, "By the law is the knowledge of sin." The law is a moral mirror, the gauge by which man can see how far he has fallen. It condemns but does not convert. It challenges but does not change. It points the finger but does not offer mercy. There is no life in the law. There is only death, for the pronouncement of the law was, "Thou shalt die." It is the "straight stick" beside which the crookedness of human nature is obvious.

There are many people who say that their religion is the Sermon on the Mount, but the man or woman is yet to be born who has ever lived up to the Sermon on the Mount. The Bible says that all have sinned and come short of His glory.

Examine your own motives before you decide that you are above reproach and living a life that absolves you from all need of conversion. Look into your own heart fearlessly and honestly before you say religious conversion is all right for some but you certainly don't stand to benefit from it.

The Universal Question

When I was preaching in Hollywood, a group of movie people asked me to talk to them about religious experiences. After my address we had a discussion period and the very first question asked was, "What is conversion?"

Some time later it was my privilege to address a group of political leaders in Washington. When the discussion period started, the first question again was, "What is conversion?"

In almost every university and college group where I have led discussions, this same question is invariably asked, "What do you mean by born again?" In my book *How to Be Born Again* (Word, 1976), I described the process this way:

> This new birth happens in all kinds of ways. It may seem to happen over a period of time or in a moment. The paths which people take to reach that point of decision may be very direct or very circuitous. Whatever the path, we

> always find Christ at the end to welcome us. And that encounter with Christ, that new birth, is the beginning of a whole new path in life under His control. Lives can be remarkably changed, marriages excitingly improved, societies influenced for good—all by the simple, sweeping surge of individuals knowing what it is to be born again.

In today's economy we hear about "born again" cars, businesses, and fashions—but that is not what I'm talking about here. Probably the simplest way to state what it means to be "born again" is to refer to it as being born into God's family.

Probably there are more different answers to this query than to almost any other pertaining to religion. What is conversion? What is involved in it? How is it accomplished? What are its effects? Why must you be converted in order to get to heaven?

The idea of conversion is certainly not unusual in our society. Any good salesman knows that he must *convert* the prospect to his particular product or way of thinking. The chief business of advertising is to *convert* the buying public from one brand to another. We speak of political leaders being *converted* from their original political philosophy and adopting a different one. During the last war, we heard a great deal about peacetime industries *converting* to war production, and most of the oil furnaces in private homes were *converted* to coal and more recently, *converted* from coal back to gas. We also talk about *converting* our money into foreign currency.

Actually the word *conversion* means "to turn around," "to change one's mind," "to turn back," or "to return." In the realm of religion it has been variously explained as "to repent," "to be regenerated," "to receive grace," "to experience religion," "to gain assurance."

I remember one confirmed alcoholic who came to one of the opening meetings of a crusade and said to me, "Mr. Graham, I'm not sure there's a word of truth in what you're saying, but I'm going to give your Christ a trial, and if He works even a little bit the way you say He will, I'll come back and sign up for life!"

Weeks later he told me that he didn't quite understand it, but every time he started to take a drink it seemed as though something or someone stopped him. Christ had given him victory over his vicious habit. He returned to his family and is now living his life for Christ. In other words, he turned around, he changed his direction, he changed his way of thinking—he had been converted!

The Nature of Conversion

Conversion can take many different forms. The way it is accomplished depends largely upon the individual—his temperament, his emotional balance, his environment, and his previous conditioning and way of life. Conversion may follow a great crisis in a person's life; or it could come after all former values have been swept away, when great disappointment has been experienced, when one has lost one's sense of power through material possessions or lost the object of one's affections. A man or woman who has been focusing all attention on financial gains or business or social prestige, or centering all affection on some one person experiences a devastating sense of loss when denied the thing that has given life its meaning.

In these tragic moments, as the individual stands

stripped of all his worldly power, when the loved one is gone beyond recall, he recognizes how terribly and completely alone he really is. In that moment, the Holy Spirit may cause the spiritual bandages to fall from his eyes and he sees clearly for the first time. He recognizes that God is the only source of real power and the only enduring fountainhead of love and companionship.

Or again, conversion may take place at the very height of personal power or prosperity—when all things are going well and the bountiful mercies of God have been bestowed generously upon you. The very goodness of God can drive you to a recognition that you owe all to God; thus, the very goodness of God leads you to repentance (Romans 2:4).

Conversion at such a moment can be as sudden and dramatic as the conversion of Paul on the road to Damascus.

Not all conversions come as a sudden, brilliant flash of soul illumination that we call a crisis conversion. There are many others that are accomplished only after a long and difficult conflict with inner motives of the person. With others, conversion comes at the climactic moment of a long period of gradual conviction of their need and revelation of the plan of salvation. This prolonged process results in conscious acceptance of Christ as personal Savior and in the yielding of life to Him.

In his spiritual autobiography, C. S. Lewis describes his conversion experience:

> You must picture me alone in that room in Magdalen, night after night, feeling, whenever my mind lifted even for a second from my work, the steady, unrelenting approach of Him whom I so earnestly desired not to meet. That which I greatly feared had at last come upon me. In

> the Trinity Term of 1929 I gave in, and admitted that God was God, and knelt and prayed: perhaps, that night, the most dejected and reluctant convert in all England. I do not then see what is now the most shining and obvious thing; the Divine humility which will accept a convert even on such terms. The Prodigal Son at least walked home on his own feet. But who can duly adore that Love which will open the high gates to a prodigal who is brought in kicking, struggling, resentful, and darting his eyes in every direction for a chance of escape? The words *compelle intrare,* "compel them to come in," have been so abused by wicked men that we shudder at them; but, properly understood, they plumb the depth of the Divine mercy. The hardness of God is kinder than the softness of men, and His compulsion is our liberation.*

We may say, therefore, that conversion can be an instantaneous event, a crisis in which the person receives a clear revelation of the love of God; or it can be a gradual unfolding accompanied by a climactic moment at the time the line is crossed between darkness and light, between death and life everlasting.

It does not always happen in exactly this way. My wife, for example, cannot remember the exact day or hour when she became a Christian, but she is certain that there was such a moment in her life, a moment when she actually crossed the line. Many young people who have grown up in Christian homes and had the benefit of Christian training are unaware of the time when they committed their lives to Christ. Someone has said we may not know the exact moment when the sun rises—but we most certainly

* From *Surprised by Joy: The Shape of My Early Life,* copyright 1966 by Harcourt, Brace, Jovanovich, pp. 228–229.

know once it has risen. Others remember very clearly when they made their public confession of faith. The reports of conversions in the New Testament indicate that most of them were the dramatic, crisis type.

Psychology Looks at Conversion

For many years, psychology left conversion and religious experience alone. In the last fifty years, however, psychologists have studied the whole process of conversion. They have pointed out that conversion is not only a Christian experience but is also found in other religions, and that it is not necessarily a religious phenomenon but also occurs in nonreligious spheres. Students of psychology have agreed that there are three steps in conversion: First, a sense of perplexity and uneasiness; second, a climax and turning point; and, third, a relaxation marked by rest and joy.

In an article entitled "Why It's Good to Feel So Bad," *The New York Times* (29 November 1983) pointed out, "Guilt, the sense of anguish that we have fallen short of our own standards, is the guardian of our goodness. It is necessary to the development of conscience in children and to the avoidance of antisocial behavior." The article goes on to explain, "In early childhood, good behavior is enforced mainly through parental introduction of guilty fear, the fear of punishment for violating a code of behavior. But as the child grows up, an 'ego ideal'—a form of father figure—becomes internalized as a model of correct behavior . . . and by adulthood, people seek to punish themselves when they betray that model. Dr. Gaylin sees the lack of appropriate role models or father figures as one cause of the growing rash of guiltless antisocial behavior among young people today." It is this feeling of guilt that creates the hunger for something better—to be found only in a right relationship to Christ.

Psychologists say that there are two kinds of conversion. One is accompanied by a violent sense of sin, and the other by a feeling of incompleteness, a struggle after a larger life and a desire for spiritual illumination.

The value of psychological studies of conversion has been underestimated. We cannot brush them aside and ignore them. Psychologists shed a great deal of light, but most of them are unwilling to accept the biblical conversion as a supernatural experience.

Actually, biblical conversion involves three steps—two of them active and one passive. In active conversion, repentance and faith are involved. Repentance is conversion viewed from its starting point, the turning from the former life. Faith indicates the objective point of conversion, the turning of God. The third, which is passive, we may call the new birth, or regeneration, commonly called being "born again," which literally means being born into God's family.

Now in order to get to heaven, Jesus said that you must be converted. I didn't say it—Jesus said it! This is not man's opinion—this is God's opinion! Jesus said, "Except ye be converted, and become as little children, ye shall not enter into the kingdom of heaven" (Matthew 18:3).

True conversion will involve the mind, the affection, and the will. There have been thousands of people who have been intellectually converted to Christ. They believe the entire Bible. They believe all about Jesus, but they have never been really converted to Him. The Bible tells us "even the devils believe and tremble" (James 2:19).

The Difference Between Intellectual Belief and Conversion

In John there is a description of the hundreds of people who were following Jesus early in His ministry. The Bible says that "many believed in his name when they saw the miracles which he did. But Jesus did not commit himself unto them" (John 2:23–24) because He knew the hearts of all men. Why would Jesus not commit Himself to them'? He knew that they believed with their heads and not with their hearts.

There is a vast difference between intellectual belief and the total conversion that saves the soul. To be sure, there must be a change in our thinking and intellectual acceptance of Christ.

There are thousands of people who have had some form of emotional experience that they refer to as conversion but who have never been truly converted to Christ. Christ demands a change in the way you live—and if your life does not conform to your experience, then you have every reason to doubt your experience! Certainly there will be a change in the elements that make up emotion when you come to Christ—hate and love will be involved, because you will begin to hate sin and love righteousness. Your affections will undergo a revolutionary change. Your devotion to Him will know no bounds. Your love for Him cannot be described.

But even if you have an intellectual acceptance of Christ, and an emotional experience—that still is not enough. There must be the conversion of the will! There must be that determination to obey and follow Christ. Your will must be bent to the will of God. Self must be nailed to the cross. Many of us can identify with the young woman who wrote us regarding this: "But I don't hang easy." None of us do, yet. Our main desire must be to please Him. It is a total commitment.

In conversion as you stand at the foot of the cross, the Holy Spirit makes you realize that you are a sinner. He directs your faith to the Christ who died in your place. You must open your heart and let Him come in. At that precise moment the Holy Spirit performs the miracle of the new birth. You actually become a new moral creature. There comes the implantation of the divine nature. You become a partaker of God's own life. Jesus Christ, through the Spirit of God, takes up residence in your heart.

Conversion is so simple that the smallest child can be converted, but it is also so profound that theologians throughout history have pondered the depth of its meaning. God has made the way of salvation so plain that "the wayfaring men, though fools, shall not err therein" (Isaiah 35:8). No person will ever be barred from the kingdom of God because he did not have the capacity to understand. The rich and the poor, the sophisticated and the simple—all can be converted.

To sum it up, conversion simply means "to change." When a person is converted he may continue to love objects which he loved before, but there will be a change of reasons for loving them. A converted person may forsake former objects of affection. He may even withdraw from his previous companions, not because he dislikes them, for many of them will be decent and amiable, but because there is more attraction for him in the fellowship of other Christians of like mind.

The converted person will love the good he once hated, and hate the sin he once loved. There will even be a change of heart about God. Where he once may have been careless about God, living in constant fear, dread, and antagonism to God, he now finds himself in a state of complete reverence, confidence, obedience, and devotion. There will be a reverential fear of God, a constant gratitude to God, a dependence upon God, and a new loyalty to Him. Before conversion there may have been gratification of the flesh. Cultural and intellectual pursuits or the making of money may have been of first and supreme importance. Now, righteousness and holiness of heart, and living the Christian life will be placed above all other concerns, for pleasing Christ will be the only goal of real importance. In other words, conversion means a complete change in the life of an individual.

A Case of Conversion

I remember so vividly a young New York career girl who came out to Los Angeles to be married. She and her fiancé had met when they were both working in a high-powered New York advertising agency, and their courtship had been conducted against a background of cocktail parties and night clubs. Filled with ambition and "on his way up," he had himself transferred to the California office, with the understanding that the girl would follow him in six months and they would be married.

About a week after she had arrived in Los Angeles, expecting to take up a joyous new life, she discovered that the man had fallen in love with a movie starlet and lacked the courage to write her about it before she left New York!

Here she was, alone in a city where she knew no one—all her plans in ruins, her pride crushed, and the future stretching ahead, bleak and empty. Her family had not been religious, and in this hour of extreme need she knew of nowhere to turn for comfort, advice, or guidance.

As she walked along the unfamiliar streets, trying to overcome her shock and humiliation, she came upon the "canvas cathedral" in which we were conducting our crusade. She said she was never sure what made her come inside, but she did, and sat glumly through the entire service. The next night she came again, and every night for the whole week, until through the cloud of bitterness and misery that surrounded her, God made His voice heard, and she came forward to confess her need of salvation.

With the burden of guilt and rejection lifted from her through faith in the Lord Jesus Christ, she came to see that the love she had lost was but a stepping stone to a far greater and much richer love. The sense of humiliation that prevented her from returning to her former New York job vanished, and rather than life being finished, she found upon her return that it was fuller than ever. Only instead of wasting her brains and organizational ability on an endless round of cocktail parties, she became extremely active walking with God and serving others.

The imagination she formerly devoted to entertaining the "office crowd" now goes into making Bible stories come alive for the young people. Her training as a fund-raiser is now being put to good use in the service of the Lord, and her minister says her ideas have been invaluable in increasing regular church attendance. Far from being rejected and unwanted, she is sought after constantly by her fellow church members. But, most important of all, her sense of loneliness has vanished, for she knows now that Jesus Christ is ever by her side, ready to comfort, to guide, and to protect her.

All this had come as a result of her conversion—her turning away from the bleak, empty, worldly road she was traveling so unhappily—to her Lord and Savior, Jesus Christ! She had found peace with God.

10

What Is Repentance?

Joy shall be in heaven over one sinner that repenteth, more than over ninety and nine just persons which need no repentance.

Luke 15:7

WE HAVE now seen that Jesus demanded conversion. We have also seen that the three elements of conversion are repentance, faith, and regeneration. It may be debatable in which order these three should come, but it is generally agreed that they probably happen at the same time. Whether you are conscious or unconscious of it, in that critical moment of conversion these three take place simultaneously.

If repentance could be described in two words, I would use the words "turning around." Turn around from what? you ask. The answer can be given in one word—"sin." The Bible teaches, as we have already seen, that sin is a transgression of the law. Sin is the rejection of all authority and the denial of all obligation to God. Sin is that evil principle which came into the Garden of Eden when Adam and Eve were tempted and fell. Ever since the disaster in Eden this evil poison has affected all men so that "all have sinned," and "there is none righteous, no, not one." Sin has destroyed our relationship with God, and as a consequence it has disturbed our relationship with each other, and even with ourselves.

We cannot possibly have peace with God or peace with each other in the world or even peace within ourselves until something is done about that "abominable thing which God hates." Not only are we told that we must renounce or turn our backs on sin, but we are also told to renounce *sins*—plural. We are to renounce the evil influence of the world, the flesh, and the devil. There can be no parleying, bargaining, compromise, or hesitation. Christ demands total loyalty.

Repentance and Faith

But here again the principle of love is involved, because when you fall in love completely and absolutely with Jesus Christ you will not want to do the things that He hates and abhors. You will automatically renounce all the sins of your life when you surrender by faith to Him. Therefore repentance and faith go hand in hand. You cannot have genuine repentance without saving faith, and you cannot have saving faith without genuine repentance.

The word *repentance* is sadly missing today from the average pulpit. It is a very unpopular word. The first sermon Jesus ever preached was "Repent: for the kingdom of heaven is at hand" (Matthew 4:17). This was God speaking through His Son. Jesus had come with a heart filled with love and compassion, but He immediately began to press home man's guilt and sins. He called upon men to acknowledge their guilt and to turn from their ungodliness. He said repentance must come before He could pour out His love, grace, and mercy upon men. Jesus refused to gloss over iniquity. He insisted upon self-judgment, upon a complete right about-face. He insisted upon a new attitude before He would reveal the love of God.

The people came to Jesus one day and told Him of certain Galileans whose blood Pilate had mingled with sacrifices as his Roman legions quelled the Jewish uprising. They reported, too, how the falling of a tower in Siloam had killed many. In answer Jesus declared, "Suppose ye that these Galileans were sinners above all the Galileans . . . I tell you, Nay: but, except ye repent, ye shall all likewise perish" (Luke 13:3). In other words, Jesus said whether men are taken away by violence, by accident, or by natural death, their doom is the same unless they have turned to God in repentance. Until this is done, faith is absolutely impossible. This does not limit the grace of God, but repentance makes way for the grace of God.

Repentance and the Grace of God

We know that salvation is based entirely upon the grace of God. The Bible says that no man is justified by the law in the sight of God, and it also says, "The just shall live by his faith" (Romans 1:17). Salvation, forgiveness, and justification are based entirely upon the atoning work of Christ. However, if the sacrifice of Christ on the cross is to be made effectual for any individual of any age, that individual must repent of sin and accept Christ by faith.

Jonah preached repentance in Nineveh until Nineveh repented. Ezekiel preached repentance when he said, "Therefore I will judge you, O house of Israel, every one according to his ways, saith the Lord God. Repent, and turn yourselves from all your transgressions; so iniquity shall not be your ruin" (Ezekiel 18:30).

The great message of John the Baptist was repentance when he said, "Repent ye: for the kingdom of heaven is at hand" (Matthew 3:2).

Repentance is mentioned seventy times in the New Testament. Jesus said, "Except ye repent, ye shall all likewise perish." The sermon that Peter preached on the Day of Pentecost was, "Repent, and be baptized every one of you in the name of Jesus Christ for the remission of sins" (Acts 2:38). Paul preached it when he said that he "testified both to the Jews, and also to the Greeks, repentance toward God, and faith toward our Lord Jesus Christ" (Acts 20:21). The Bible says God commands repentance, "And the times of this ignorance God winked at; but now commandeth all men everywhere to repent" (Acts 17:30). It is a command. It is an imperative. God says. "Repent! Or perish!" Have you repented? Are you sure of it?

There are many biblical examples of false repentance. For example, Pharaoh said to the children of Israel who were seeking to leave Egypt for the promised land, "I have sinned . . ." (Exodus 9:27). Obviously it was an expression of regret or remorse but not an expression of true repentance. Saul did the same thing in 1 Samuel 15:24, 30 and 26:21. But when David said to the prophet Nathan, "I have sinned" in 2 Samuel 12:13 and 20:10, 17, he was truly repentant (see Psalm 51).

Jesus' Definition of Repentance

What did Jesus mean by the word *repent?* Why does it appear over and over throughout the Bible? If you look in a modern dictionary you will find that repent means "to feel sorry for, or to regret." But the original words that Jesus spoke meant a great deal more than that. They meant a great deal more than just regretting and feeling sorry about sin. The biblical word *repent* means "to change, or to turn." It is a word of power and action. It is a word that signifies a complete turnabout in the individual. When the Bible calls upon us to repent of sin, it means that we should turn away from sin, that we should do an about-face and walk in the opposite direction from sin and all that it implies.

Jesus told the parable of the Prodigal Son to dramatize what He meant by the word *repent.* When the Prodigal Son repented he didn't just sit still and feel sorry about all his sins. He wasn't passive and limp about it. He didn't stay where he was, surrounded by the swine. He got up and left! He turned his feet in the other direction. He sought out his father and humbled himself before him, and then he was forgiven.

Too many modern Christians have lost sight of what the Bible means when it talks about repentance. They think that repentance is little more than shaking their heads over their sins and saying, "My, but I'm sorry I did that!" and then continuing to live just as they have lived before.

True repentance means "to change, to turn away from, to go in a new direction." To be sorry is not enough in repentance. Judas was sorry enough to hang himself. It was an admission of guilt without true repentance. Even reformation is not enough. There is no torture that you can give your body, no trials you can set for your mind that will be pleasing to Almighty God. Our sins were atoned for by Christ on the cross. There He suffered sin's penalty. No suffering that we can undergo will lead us to repentance.

Repentance Is Not Mere Emotion

When I speak of repentance I am not speaking of the oldtime mourners' bench. Many people have taught that to repent you must mourn for a stated time in order to be ready for salvation. One man told me the night he found Christ he went forward in an old-fashioned camp meeting some years ago. While he was kneeling at the altar trying to find God, some dear sister came and slapped him on the back and said, "Hold on, brother! If you want God, you'll have to hold on." A few minutes later a church officer came up and slapped him across the back and said, "Brother, turn loose!" Then another sister came up a few minutes later and said, "The night I was converted a big light hit me in the face and knocked me cold." He said, "I tried to turn loose and hold on at the same time while looking for the light. I almost never made it in the confusion!"

A very intelligent Christian leader once told me that at the time he was converted the demonstration of emotion expected of him by the preacher and congregation almost kept him from coming to God.

Falsely produced emotionalism in some revival meetings has been a stumbling block to many a sincere, searching soul. But the type of repentance I'm talking about is true biblical repentance, which involves three things: it involves the *intellect*, the *emotion*, and the *will*.

Three Aspects of Repentance

First, there must be a knowledge of sin. The Bible says, "All have sinned, and come short of the glory of God" (Romans 3:23). When Isaiah was convicted of his sins he said, " Woe is me! . . . I am a man of unclean lips" (Isaiah 6:5). When Job got a glimpse of God's holiness he said, "I abhor myself" (Job 42:6). When Peter was convicted of his sins he said, "I am a sinful man" (Luke 5:8). When Paul was convicted of his sins he called himself "the chief of sinners" (1 Timothy 1:15).

It is the Holy Spirit who brings about this conviction. Actually, repentance cannot take place unless first there is a movement of the Holy Spirit in the heart and mind. The Holy Spirit may use a mother's prayers, a pastor's sermon, a Christian radio program, the sight of a church steeple, or the death of a loved one to bring about this necessary conviction. However, I have seen men in some of our meetings stand trembling under conviction and still not repent of their sins. It is possible to be convicted of sin and know you are a sinner and even shed tears over your sins, and yet not repent.

Second, the *emotions* are involved in repentance, just as they are in all genuine experiences. Paul said there is a godly sorrow that worketh toward repentance. Someone has said, "Many people abhor all emotion, and some critics are suspicious of any conversion that does not take place in a refrigerator. There are many dangers in false emotionalism, produced for its own effect, but that does not rule out true emotion and depth of feeling."

As Dr. W. E. Sangster, the great British Methodist preacher, says in his book, *Let Me Commend,* "The man who screams at a football or baseball game but is distressed when he hears of a sinner weeping at the cross and murmurs something about the dangers of emotionalism hardly merits intelligent respect."

Horace Walpole once accused John Wesley of acting out very ugly emotionalism in his preaching, yet Wesley turned thousands to God.

Third, repentance involves the *will*.

It is only when we come to the will that we find the very heart of repentance. There must be that determination to forsake sin—to change one's attitudes toward self, toward sin, and toward God; to change one's feeling; to change one's will, disposition, and purpose.

Only the Spirit of God can give you the determination necessary for true repentance. It means more than the little girl who prayed, "Make me good—not real good, but good enough so I won't get whipped."

There are thousands of people in America who have their names on church rolls. They go to church when it is convenient. They give their money to the church and support its activities. They shake hands with the minister after the service and tell him what a splendid sermon he preached. They may talk the language of the Christian and many of them can quote a fair amount of Scripture, but they have never really experienced true repentance. They have a sort of "I can take-it-or-leave-it-alone" attitude toward religion. They turn to God and pray when they get in a tight place, but the rest of the time they do not give God very much thought. The Bible teaches that when a person comes to Christ a change takes place that is reflected in everything he does.

Repentance Demands Surrender

There is not one verse of Scripture that indicates you can be a Christian and live any kind of a life you want to. When Christ enters into the human heart, He expects to be Lord and Master. He commands complete surrender. He demands control of your intellectual processes. He requires that your body be subject to Him. He expects you to surrender your talents and abilities to Him. He expects nothing less than that all your work and labor will be performed in His name.

Too many of today's professing Christians would give up going to church before they would give up getting a new refrigerator. Given a choice between making the down payment on a new car or contributing to the building of a new Sunday school, it is easy to guess what the decision of many would be. Thousands of so-called Christians are putting money and the things that make up our high standard of living ahead of the teachings of Christ. We can find time for the movies, baseball, or football games, but we can't find time for God. We can save toward a new home or a bigger television set, but we feel we no longer can afford to tithe. This is idolatry.

A change must take place! We point our fingers at the heathen and at the idol worshipers of old, but the only difference is that our graven images are made of gleaming chromium and steel and have thermostats and defrosting devices instead of jeweled eyes! Instead of gold, their surfaces are covered with easy-to-clean lifetime porcelain, but we worship them just the same and feel that our lives would be impossible without them. We have come to worship things, status, fame, popularity, money, security. Anything that comes between God and ourselves is idolatry.

Jesus demands Lordship over all such things. He wants you to yield everything concerning your social life, your family life, your business life to Him. He must have first place in everything you do or think or say, for when you truly repent you turn toward God in everything.

We have the warning of Christ that He will not receive us into His kingdom until we are ready to give up all, until we are ready to turn from all sin in our lives. Don't try to do it part way. Don't say, "I'll give up some of my sins and hang on to some others. I'll live part of my life for Jesus and part for my own desires." Jesus expects one hundred percent surrender, and when that is accomplished He rewards a thousandfold. But don't expect Jesus to hand out any five hundred percent awards for fifty percent surrenders! God doesn't work that way. He demands all. When you have determined that you are renouncing sin, forsaking sin, and yielding all to Christ, you have taken another step toward peace with God.

The repentant thief on the cross said to Jesus, "Lord, remember me . . ." (Luke 23:42). His use of the word "Lord" implied his total submission to Jesus Christ. It implied his total surrender and true conversion. This is the result of true repentance.

With the hymnwriter, the repentant sinner says:

All to Jesus I surrender, All to Him I freely give;
I will ever love and trust Him, in His presence daily live.
All to Jesus I surrender, make me, Savior, wholly Thine.
Let me feel the Holy Spirit, Truly know that Thou art mine.

11

What Is Faith?

For by grace are ye saved through faith; and that not of yourselves: it is the gift of God: not of works, lest any man should boast.

Ephesians 2:8, 9

WE ARE now ready to take up the next step in finding peace with God. You are now ready to forsake your past sinful life. You are determined that this change is going to take place in your life. You are no longer headed away from God, but you are moving toward His love and mercy and protection. You have made your decision. You have repented; you have chosen the right road, even though it may be a difficult one. You have chosen the road that Moses took almost 3,500 years ago when he renounced his right to the throne of Egypt and decided in favor of God!

Moses was forty years old when he fled Egypt for fear of his life. Forty years later he came back to lead the Israelites out of Egypt. What had changed? He had made his great decision. He concluded that faith and truth in company with agony and hardship were better than wealth and fame and the absence of God's love. Few men in history have been called upon to make a more difficult decision than his.

A Man of Faith

Moses was a man of education and culture, a man of wealth and prominence. As the son of Pharaoh's daughter he had been accustomed to every honor, every luxury, and every privilege. The throne of Egypt, the richest, most powerful, most spectacularly successful country of its time, was within his grasp.

Yet the Bible records that "By faith Moses, when he was come to years, refused to be called the son of Pharaoh's daughter; Choosing rather to suffer affliction with the people of God, than to enjoy the pleasures of sin for a season; Esteeming the reproach of Christ greater riches than the treasures in Egypt: for he had respect unto the recompense of the reward. By faith he forsook Egypt, not fearing the wrath of the king: for he endured, as seeing him who is invisible" (Hebrews 11:24–27). This passage was referring to Moses after his forty years in the wilderness with God—not the fiery young murderer who fled from Pharaoh in fear of his life.

Notice, it says that he "refused" and he "forsook"—this is true repentance. And then it says he did it "by faith"! This is the next step—*faith*. Moses made this decision not in a moment of overt emotionalism that some psychologists insist is necessary for religious experience. He was not motivated by frustration. He was not a hopeless misfit or an unfulfilled man. Moses was not choosing the path of God as a compensation for the rewards that he felt life had withheld from him, nor was he turning to the religious life out of boredom and apathy. He did not want for interest, entertainment, and amusement.

A Matter of Choice

None of these arguments, or the many others so often advanced as reasons for seeking life with God, were valid in the case of Moses. He was not forced to run from the flesh and the devil. He did it from choice. Moses was certainly neither weak-minded nor weak-willed. He was not a child clinging to the security of an established order. He was not a nonentity seeking recognition and prestige. He was not any of the things that those who mock religion say one must be to feel the need of salvation. Moses had even more than the dreams to which most men would aspire; and yet out of his mature judgment in the prime of life he turned his back on wealth, position, and esteem and chose instead faith in God.

Every time I hear it said that only the hopeless and helpless, only the maladjusted need the comfort of "religion," I think of Moses.

It has been my privilege to talk to many men and women concerning their spiritual problems. I have learned that when men and women of sound judgment reject Christ as their Lord and Master, they do it not because they find Christian doctrines intellectually distasteful, but because they seek to avoid the responsibilities and obligations that the Christian life demands. Their faint hearts rather than their brilliant minds stand between them and Christ. They are not willing to submit themselves and surrender everything to Christ.

It is interesting to note that the two men most used of

God in the Bible (one in the Old Testament and one in the New) were also the two best educated: Moses and Paul.

Moses considered the claims and obligations of God carefully. At forty he fled, a murderer. At eighty, he returned—a leader. He realized that if he was to embrace God he would have to do it at the sacrifice of the things that men usually hold most dear. He made no hasty examination. He came to no half-considered conclusions under sudden impulse or emotional reaction. He knew how much was at stake, and he arrived at his decision with the full use of his well-trained and superior mental faculties. His final choice was not in the nature of a temporary experiment. He did not select faith as a tentative measure. It was a mature conviction with an unalterable purpose, a conviction not to be shaken by changes of fortune or the trials of long-endured privation. He carefully burned all the bridges and ships that might have made retreat possible from his new position. When Moses had his great crisis moment at the age of eighty, he committed himself totally and without reservation for all time and under all circumstances to God and His commands.

How different was the quality of Moses' decision from that of the famous biographer Gamaliel Bradford, who as he neared the end of his life said, "I do not dare read the New Testament for fear of awakening a storm of anxiety and doubt and dread, of having taken the wrong path, of having been a traitor to the plain and simple God."

Moses had no such fear. And neither should you fear if you turn yourself wholeheartedly to Christ now and forever *by faith*. Don't turn to Him saying, "I'll try Christianity for a while. If it works I'll go on with it, but if it doesn't I still have time to choose another way of life." When you come to Christ, every bridge has to be burned behind you, with no thought of ever turning back.

They Turned Back on Their Boats

Years ago, when the wings of the fierce Roman eagle cast an ominous shadow over the world, those audacious warriors whom Caesar led set out to conquer Britain. As the enemy vessels appeared on the horizon, thousands of Englishmen bravely gathered on the heights to defend their homeland. To their amazement, the tides and the sea destroyed most of the Roman ships. Thus the only avenue of retreat was cut off for the daring invaders. They fought with wild abandon, their escape route cut off. With such an indomitable spirit, how could they fail to conquer! Little wonder the petty village on the banks of the Tiber became the Mistress of the world!

Just so, Christ will accept nothing less than complete surrender and absolute devotion. "And Jesus said unto him, 'No man, having put his hand to the plow, and looking back, is fit for the kingdom of God'" (Luke 9:62).

Moses made his soul-shaking choice as he stood at the fork of life's highway. His judicial mind weighed all the facts that bore upon his decision. He looked long and carefully down each road to its termination. He considered all the pros and cons and only then did he decide to put his trust and faith in God.

Moses Burned His Bridges

First he looked down the broad road, the bright road filled with power and luxury, filled with gaiety and wine, rich in the things the world counts as pleasure. It was a familiar road. He knew it well. He had traveled it for forty years and he knew that it ended in destruction, knew that it could only lead to hell.

Then Moses looked down the other road, the narrow road, the more difficult road. He saw the suffering, the affliction, the humiliation and disappointment. He saw the hardships and the trials, the sorrows and the pains, but by *faith* he saw also the triumphs and the reward of eternal life.

A man of lesser judgment, a man of lesser experience than Moses, might have been tempted to take the first road. Egypt was then the greatest power on earth. It held command of the fertile Nile valley, the granary of the world. Its armies were invincible, its colleges and universities were setting the pattern that other centuries would follow.

Few of us are ever asked to give up as much for God as Moses did. Few of us are ever shown temptation in such abundance and variety and asked to withstand it. Few of us have such earthly delights and pleasures spread before our eyes, and even the Scriptures admit that there is pleasure in sin, if only for a season. The pleasure is fleeting and leaves no comfort in its wake.

In choosing God, Moses made a great sacrifice, but he also won a great reward. Great fortunes were rare in Moses' time, and few men indeed had the opportunity that he had to become the wealthiest man on earth.

The Wealth of the World

Today, many men can amass great fortunes. In 1923 (when fortune gathering was this country's major interest) a group of the world's most successful financiers gathered at the

Edgewater Beach Hotel in Chicago. Even in the fabulous twenties, the meeting was an impressive array of wealth and power. Seated at a single table were the president of the world's largest independent steel company, the president of the largest utility company, the president of the New York Stock Exchange, a member of the cabinet of the president of the United States, the president of the Bank of International Settlements, the man who was known as the biggest trader on Wall Street, and another who headed the world's most powerful monopoly. Together, these men controlled more wealth than the United States Treasury! Their success stories were known to every schoolboy. They were the models whom other men tried to copy. They were the financial and industrial giants of America!

In 1923 the widely publicized stories of these men were glamorous and exciting. They fired the imagination! They kindled envy! They inspired other men to try to be as they were! But in 1923 their stories were only half told—the closing chapters were yet to be written.

At the time these eight men sat down together at the hotel in Chicago they were each at the place in their individual lives where Moses had been when he stood at the crossroads. These men were at the crossroads also, and two paths stretched out before each of them. Perhaps they were paths they could not see, paths about which they did not care. Certainly they were paths they didn't choose to follow, and today their stories are complete. Today we know those final chapters. We can review their lives, just as we can review the life of Moses, and see which seems the wisest and the best.

Charles Schwab, president of the steel company, lived the last years of his life on borrowed money and died penniless.

Arthur Cutten, greatest of the wheat speculators, died abroad insolvent. Richard Whitney, president of the New York Stock Exchange, served a term in Sing-Sing Penitentiary. Albert Fall, the cabinet member, was pardoned from prison so he could die at home. Jessie Livermore, the "bear" of Wall Street; Leon Frazer, president of the Bank of International Settlements; and Ivon Kreuger, head of the world's largest monopoly, all committed suicide!

These men all had money, power, fame, prestige, intelligence, and education—but every one of them lacked the one attribute that gives life its real meaning and purpose. They lacked the one attribute that is essential to the Christian creed and conduct—the attribute that makes conversion possible, that makes regeneration real. They refused to believe! Compare their lives with those of missionaries who have left all to follow Christ. They may die penniless and in pain, but they have died *for* something!

These wealthy men had no faith, or if they did have faith, they refused to act upon it. How different the closing chapters of their lives would have been if they had been able to count faith in Christ among their treasuries.

Moses Turned His Back on the World's Wealth

Notice it was through *faith* that Moses renounced the wealth of Egypt. It was his *faith* that made him know that even though he might suffer privation and humiliation all the rest of his life on earth, in the end he would receive the greatest of rewards—eternal life.

Men like Cutten and Schwab might have thought Moses a fool. They would have said, "A bird in the hand is worth far more than two in the bush." They would have said, "Look, you know what you have in Egypt. You know what a man of your brains can do to manipulate this wealth and power. Play your cards right and Egypt will control the world. You can put all the lesser countries out of business. You can get rid of all the competition and run things your own way." That's what they would have said, because that's the way they thought, that's the way they operated, that's the way many of them amassed their fortunes. They would have laughed at a person who said he believed God or had faith in Christ. They would have said, "Faith isn't good business. It isn't smart."

The Bible teaches that faith is the only approach to God. "For he that cometh to God must believe that he is, and that he is a rewarder of them that diligently seek him" (Hebrews 11:6). The Bible also teaches that faith pleases God more than anything else. "Without faith it is impossible to please him" (Hebrews 11:6).

People all over the world torture themselves, clothe themselves in strange garments, disfigure their bodies, deny themselves the necessities of life, spend much time in prayer and self-sacrifice in an effort to make themselves acceptable in God's sight. This may be all well and good, but the greatest thing we can do to please God is to believe Him.

I might go to a friend and flatter him, but, if after all my flowery phrases I were to tell him I did not believe him, every flattering thing I said would have been in vain. I would have built him up only to let him down.

Belief Is Essential

The greatest way we can please God is to *believe* His Word. It would seem that Christ was almost pleading for faith on the part of His hearers when He said, "Believe me that I am in the Father, and the Father in me: or else believe me for the very works' sake" (John 14:11).

The Bible declares that *faith* is absolutely essential. You ask, "Well, if faith is so important, what is faith? What do you mean by faith? What is a definition of faith? How can I know if I have proper faith? How much faith must I have?"

Wait just a minute—not so many questions at a time! I'll try to answer them as we go along.

The Bible teaches, time and time again, that we can have salvation only through faith:

"*Believe* on the Lord Jesus Christ, and thou shalt be saved, and thy house" (Acts 16:31).

"But as many as received him, to them gave he power to become the sons of God, even to them that *believe* on his name" (John 1:12).

"And by him all that *believe* are justified from all things, from which ye could not be justified by the law of Moses" (Acts 13:39).

"But to him that worketh not, but *believeth* on him that justifieth the ungodly, his faith is counted for righteousness" (Romans 4:5).

"Therefore being justified by *faith*, we have peace with God through our Lord Jesus Christ" (Romans 5:1).

"But we are not of them who draw back unto perdition; but of them that *believe* to the saving of the soul" (Hebrews 10:39).

"For by grace are ye saved through *faith*; and that not of yourselves: it is the gift of God" (Ephesians 2:8).

The Nature of Faith

Are we actually saved by faith? No, we're saved by grace *through faith*. Faith is simply the channel through which God's grace to us is received. It is the hand that reaches out and receives the gift of His love. In Hebrews 11:1, we read, "Now faith is the substance of things hoped for, the evidence of things not seen." Weymouth has translated it this way, which makes it easier to understand, "Now faith is a confident assurance of that for which we hope, a conviction of the reality of things which we do not see." Faith literally means "to give up, surrender, or commit." Faith is complete confidence.

I have never been to the North Pole, and yet I believe there is a North Pole. How do I know? I know because somebody told me. I read about it in a history book, I saw a map in a geography book, and I believe the men who wrote those books. I accept it by faith.

The Bible says, "Faith cometh by hearing, and hearing by the word of God" (Romans 10:17). We believe what God has to say about salvation. We accept it without question.

Martin Luther has translated Hebrews 11:27 this way, "For he held on to Him whom he saw not just as though he saw Him."

It is not some peculiar, mysterious quality for which we must strive. Jesus said we must become as little children, and just as little children trust their parents, so we must trust God.

Suppose I were driving along the road at fifty miles an hour and I came to the crest of a hill. Would I immediately slam on my brakes, stop my car, get out, walk up to the top of the hill, and look over to see if the road continues? No, I wouldn't do that. I would trust the highway department of the particular state in which I was driving. I would continue at my normal rate of speed, secure in the knowledge that the road continued on ahead even though I couldn't see it. I would accept it on faith. So it is with saving faith in Christ!

Three Aspects of Faith

Again, as in repentance, there are three things involved in faith. First, there must be a *knowledge* of what God has said. That's why it's so important for you to read the Bible. That's why it's important for you to know something of the teaching of the Bible concerning the salvation of the soul. Just to know that you are a sinner and that Christ died for you is enough knowledge. Knowing no more than John 3:16 could be enough knowledge. Many have been converted on less. But on anything as important as this you should be as well informed as possible, and the only place to learn about salvation is in the Bible!

Many people say, "But I cannot understand much of the Bible, therefore I don't try to read it." That is not the wise attitude. There are many things in the Bible that I do not understand. My finite mind will never understand all about the infinite. I do not understand all about television, but I do not refuse to turn on my television set. I accept it by faith.

But God does not ask the impossible. He does not ask you to take a leap in the dark concerning conversion. Believing in Christ is based on the best evidence in the world, the Bible. Even though you do not understand it all, you can accept it at face value because God said it. One of the first attacks the devil makes on man is to get him to doubt the Word of God: "Yea, hath God said?" (Genesis 3:1). If you begin doubting and putting question marks over God's Word, then you're in trouble. There must be a knowledge that you are a sinner. You must have the knowledge that

Christ died for your sins and that He rose again for your justification. The death, burial, and resurrection of Jesus Christ is the very heart of the Gospel. That must be believed and accepted as a minimum for conversion.

Second, the *emotions* again are involved. The Bible says, "The fear of the Lord is the beginning of wisdom" (Proverbs 1:7). Paul said, "The love of Christ constraineth us" (2 Corinthians 5:14). Desire, love, fear—all are emotions. Emotion cannot be cut out of life. No intelligent person would think of saying, "Let's do away with all emotion." To remove all personality from deep feeling is impossible. We cannot imagine life without the warm overtones of feeling. Suppose we had a family where everyone acted only from a cold sense of duty. Suppose I asked my wife to marry me after I had explained to her first of all that I had no feelings for her at all.

As Dr. Sangster says, "Carry the same principle over into religion. Require that the Herald of God announce the offer of His King, freely to pardon and fully to bless, but firmly forbid that any transport of joy should accompany either the announcement of the news or its glad reception, and you ask the impossible."

There is going to be a tug at the heart. Emotion may vary in religious experience. Some people are stoical and others are demonstrative, but the feeling will be there.

When Churchill gave his masterful speeches to the British people during the war, he appealed to logic, but at the same time he made his audience *feel*. I remember hearing him one time in Glasgow. He challenged my thinking, but he made me feel like standing up and shouting and waving a flag! When you fall in love with Jesus Christ your emotions are bound to be stirred.

Third, and most important of all, is the *will*. It's like three little men—one is named "Intellect," the second is named "Emotion," and the third is named "Will." Intellect says that the gospel is logical. Emotion puts pressure upon Will and says, "I feel love for Christ," or "I feel fear of judgment." And then the middleman, called Will, is the referee. He sits there with his hand on his chin, in deep thought, trying to make up his mind. It is actually the *will* that makes the final and lasting decision. It is possible to have the intellectual conviction and the emotional feeling and still not be properly converted to Christ. Faith has legs. "Faith without works is dead" (James 2:20).

An Example of Faith

I heard about a man some years ago who was rolling a wheelbarrow back and forth across Niagara River on a tightrope. Thousands of people were shouting him on. He put a two-hundred-pound sack of dirt in the wheelbarrow and rolled it over, and then he rolled it back. Then he turned to the crowd and said, "How many of you believe that I can roll a man across?"

Everybody shouted! One man in the front row was very excited in his professed belief. The man pointed to this excited professor and said, "You're next!"

You couldn't see that man for dust! He actually didn't believe it. He said he believed it, he thought he believed it—but he was not willing to get in the wheelbarrow.

Just so with Christ. There are many people who say they believe on Him, who say they will follow Him. But they never have gotten into the wheelbarrow. They actually never have committed and surrendered themselves wholly, one hundred percent to Christ.

There are many people who ask, "Well, how much faith does it take?" Jesus said only the faith as of "a grain of mustard seed."

Others ask, "What kind of faith?" It is not a matter of any special kind of faith. There is only one kind, really. It is the *object* of the faith that counts. What is the object of your faith? The object of your faith must be Christ. Not faith in ritual, not faith in sacrifices, not faith in morals, not faith in yourself—not faith in anything but Christ!

Now the Bible teaches that faith will manifest itself in three ways. It will manifest itself in doctrine—in what you believe. It will manifest itself in worship—your communion with God and the fellowship of the church. It will manifest itself in morality—in the way you live and behave, which we will discuss in other chapters.

The Bible also teaches that faith does not end with trust in Christ for your salvation. Faith continues. Faith grows. It may be weak at first, but it will become stronger as you begin to read the Bible, pray, go to church, and experience God's faithfulness in your Christian life. After you have repented of sins and accepted Him by faith, then you must trust Him to keep you, strengthen you, enable you, sustain you. You will learn more and more how to rely on Christ for every need, in meeting every circumstance and every trial. You will learn to say with Paul, "I am crucified with Christ; nevertheless I live; yet not I, but Christ liveth in me: and the life which I now live in the flesh I live by the faith of the Son of God, who loved me, and gave himself for me" (Galatians 2:20).

When you have saving faith in Jesus Christ, you have taken an additional step toward having peace with God.

12

The Old and the New

Except a man be born again he cannot see the kingdom of God.

John 3:3

IF I could come and have a heart-to-heart chat with you in your living room, you perhaps would turn to me and confess, "I am perplexed, confused, and mixed up. I have transgressed God's laws. I have lived contrary to His commandments. I thought I could get along without God's help. I have tried to make up my own rules and I've failed. The bitter lessons that I've learned have come through suffering and tragic experience. What wouldn't I give to be born again! What wouldn't I give to be able to go back and start all over—what a different road I'd travel if I could!"

If those words strike a familiar chord in your heart, if they echo the thoughts that have been moving through your mind, I want to tell you some glorious news. Jesus said you can be born anew! You can have the fresh and better start for which you've prayed. You can lose your despised and sinful self and step forth a new person, a clean and peaceful being from whom sin has been washed away.

A Way Out

No matter how soiled your past, no matter how snarled your present, no matter how hopeless your future seems to be—there is a way out. There is a sure, safe, everlasting way out—but there is only one! You have only one choice to make. You have only one path to follow, other than the torturous, unrewarding path you've been treading.

You can go on being miserable, discontented, frightened, unhappy, and disgusted with yourself and your life; or you can decide right now that you want to be born again. You can decide right now to wipe out your sinful past and make a new start, a fresh start, a right start. You can decide now to become the person that Jesus promised you could be.

How Do I Find It?

The next logical question that you may ask is, "How can I have this rebirth? How can I be born again? How can I start afresh?"

This is the question that Nicodemus asked Jesus that night two thousand years ago under an Oriental sky. Being born again, however, means a great deal more than just a fresh start, or turning over a new leaf, or reforming. As we have already seen, the Bible teaches that you were born the first time into the physical world but your spiritual nature was born in sin. The Bible declares that you are "dead in trespasses and sins" (Ephesians 2:1).

The Bible teaches that there is nothing in your dead and sinful nature that can originate life. Being dead in sin, you cannot produce a life of righteousness. Many people are trying to produce a good, holy, and righteous life without being born again, but they can do nothing but fail. A corpse cannot reproduce. The Bible teaches that "sin, when it is finished, bringeth forth death" (James 1:15). All of us are dead spiritually.

Your old nature cannot serve God. The Bible says, "The natural man receiveth not the things of the Spirit of God . . . neither can he know them" (1 Corinthians 2:14). In our natural state we are actually at enmity with God. We are not subject to the laws of God, neither indeed can we be, according to Romans 8:7.

The Bible also teaches that our old nature is totally corrupt. From its head to its feet "there is no soundness in it"; it is full of "wounds, and bruises, and petrifying sores" (Isaiah 1:6). Its heart is "deceitful above all things, and desperately wicked" (Jeremiah 17:9). It is corrupt, subject to deceitful lust.

The Bible also teaches that our old nature is a self-nature. It is incapable of being renovated. The Bible teaches that when we are born again, we put off the old man—we do not patch him up. The old self is to be crucified, not cultivated. Jesus said the cleansing of the outside of the cup and the platter leaves the inside just as dirty as before.

You Must Be Born Again!

The Bible also teaches that unless we have experienced this new birth we cannot get into the kingdom of heaven. Jesus made it even stronger. He said, "Ye must be born again" (John 3:7). There is nothing indefinite, nothing optional about that. He who would enter the kingdom of God must be born again.

Salvation is not just repairing the original self. It is a new self created of God in righteousness and true holiness. Regeneration is not even a change of nature, or a change of heart. Being born again is not a change—it is a regeneration, a new generation. It is a second birth. "Ye must be born again."

There is nothing about the old nature that God will accept. There is no soundness in it. The old nature is too weak to follow Christ. Paul said, "Ye cannot do the things that ye would" (Galatians 5:17). Those who are in the flesh cannot serve God. "Doth a fountain send forth at the same place sweet water and bitter? Can the fig tree, my brethren, bear olive berries?" asked James (James 3:11, 12).

The old man is described in Romans as "Their throat is an open sepulchre; with their tongues they have used deceit; the poison of asps is under their lips: Whose mouth is full of cursing and bitterness: Their feet are swift to shed blood: Destruction and misery are in their ways: . . . There is no fear of God before their eyes" (Romans 3:13–18).

How are you going to reform or patch up or change such throats and tongues and lips and feet and eyes as these? It is impossible. Jesus, knowing that it was impossible to change, patch up, and reform, said you must have a total new birth, "Ye must be born again." Jesus said, "That which is born of the flesh is flesh." On another occasion the Bible says, "Can the Ethiopian change his skin, or the leopard change his spots?" (Jeremiah 13:23). Again in Romans the Bible says, "They that are in the flesh cannot please God." "In me (that is, in my flesh) dwelleth no good thing" (Romans 7:18). Again the Bible says, "Without holiness no man shall see the Lord" (Hebrews 12:14).

The life that comes from the new birth cannot be obtained by natural development or self-effort. Man does not by nature have this holiness that God requires for heaven. In the new birth alone is the beginning of such a life to be found. To live the life of God we must have the nature of God.

What God Does

The whole matter of receiving new life is like a coin. A coin has two sides. The receiving of new life has a divine side and a human side. We have seen the human side in our chapter on conversion, we have seen what we must do. Now let's see what God does.

Being born again is altogether a work of the Holy Spirit. There is nothing we can do to obtain this new birth. The Bible says, "But as many as received him, to them gave he power to become the sons of God, even to them that believed on his name: Which were born, not of blood, nor of the will of the flesh, nor of the will of man, but of God" (John 1:12–13). In other words, we cannot be born of blood; that means we cannot inherit the new birth. God has no grandchildren.

We cannot inherit Christianity. We might have had a Christian father and mother, but that does not necessarily produce a Christian child. I could be born in a garage, but that doesn't make me an automobile! God has no grandchildren.

We cannot be born of the will of the flesh, the Scripture says. In other words, there is nothing we can do about it. The unbeliever is dead. A dead man has no life to do anything.

Nor can one be born of the will of man. This new birth cannot be produced by human devices or schemes. Many people think they are automatically born again when they join a church or go through some religious ritual or make some New Year's resolution or give a large gift to an outstanding charitable institution. All of these are fine and right, but they do not produce the new birth.

A Divine Work

Jesus told us we must be born again. The infinitive *be* is passive. It shows that it is something that must be done for us. No man can "born" himself. He must *be* born. The new birth is wholly foreign to our will. In other words, the new birth is a divine work—we are born of God.

Nicodemus could not understand how he could be born the second time. In perplexity he asked twice, "How?"

Even though the new birth seems mysterious, that does not make it untrue. We may not understand the how of electricity, but we know that it lights our homes, runs our television and radio sets. We do not understand how the sheep grows wool, the cow grows hair, or the fowl grows feathers—but we know they do. We do not understand many mysteries, but we accept by faith the fact that at the moment we repent of sin and turn by faith to Jesus Christ we are born again.

It is the infusion of divine life into the human soul. It is the implantation or impartation of divine nature into the human soul whereby we become the children of God. We receive the breath of God. Christ through the Holy Spirit takes up residence in our hearts. We are attached to God for eternity. That means that if you have been born again you will live as long as God lives, because you are now sharing His very life. The long lost fellowship man had with God in the Garden of Eden has been restored.

The Results of the New Birth

When you are born again several results follow: First, it will increase your vision and *understanding*. The Bible says, "God, who commanded the light to shine out of darkness, hath shined in our hearts, to give the light of the knowledge of the glory of God in the face of Jesus Christ" (2 Corinthians 4:6). Again the Bible says, "The eyes of your understanding being enlightened" (Ephesians 1:18). Things that you used to laugh at as foolishness you now accept by faith. Your whole mental process is changed. God becomes the hub of your intellectual thinking. He becomes the center. The ego has been dethroned.

Second, your *heart* undergoes a revolution. The Bible says, "A new spirit will I put within you: and I will take away the stony heart out of your flesh, and I will give you an heart of flesh" (Ezekiel 36:26).

Your affections have undergone a radical change. Your new nature loves God and the things pertaining to God. You love the finest and highest things in life. You reject the lower and baser. You discover a new appreciation for the social problems around you. Your heart beats with compassion for those who are less fortunate.

Third, your *will* undergoes a tremendous change. Your determinations are different. Your motives are changed. The Bible says, "Now the God of Peace . . . make you perfect in every good work to do his will, working in you that which is well-pleasing in his sight" (Hebrews 13:20, 21).

This new nature that you receive from God is bent to

the will of God. You will want to do only His will. You are utterly and completely devoted to Him. There is a new self-determination, inclination, disposition, a new principle of living, new choices. You seek to glorify God. You seek fellowship with other Christians in the church. You love the Bible. You love to spend time in prayer with God. Your whole disposition is changed. Whereas your life once was filled with unbelief, the root and foundation of all sin, and you once doubted God, now you believe Him. Now you have utmost confidence and faith in God and His Word.

There may have been a time when pride was the very center of your life. You had ambitious thoughts of yourself, your powers, desires, and aims; but now that will begin to change. There may have been a time when there was hatred in your life. Envy, discontent, and malice filled your thoughts toward others. That, too, will gradually change.

There was a time when you could easily tell a lie. There were falsehoods and hypocrisies in many of your thoughts, words, and deeds. That is now all changed. There was a time when you gave in to the lust of the flesh. That is now changed. You have been born again. You may stumble into some of these traps that the devil puts out for you, but immediately you will be sorry, confess your sins, and ask forgiveness, because you have been born again. Your very nature has changed.

The Pig and the Lamb

There is an old story about the pig and the lamb. The farmer brought the pig into the house. He gave him a bath, polished his hoofs, put some Chanel No. 5 on him, tied a ribbon around his neck, and placed him in the living room.

The pig looked fine. He almost seemed to be acceptable to society and to friends who might come in, he was so fresh and clean. He made a very nice and companionable pet for a few minutes. But as soon as the door was opened, the pig left the living room and jumped into the first mud puddle he could find. Why? Because he was still a pig at heart. His nature had not been changed. He had been changed outwardly but not inwardly.

Take a lamb, on the other hand. Put a lamb in a living room and then turn him out into the yard, and he will try his best to avoid all mud puddles. Why? Because his nature is that of a lamb.

You can take a man—dress him up, put him in the front row in church, and he almost looks like a saint. He may fool even his best friends for a while, but then put him in his office the next day, or put him at home or put him in the club on Saturday night, and you will see his true nature come out again. Why does he act that way? Because his nature has not been changed. He has not been born again.

The Meaning of Justification

Now the moment you receive the new birth, the moment you are born again, the moment you receive this divine impartation of a new nature, you are justified in the sight of God. By being justified is meant "just-as-if-I'd" never sinned. Justification is that act of God whereby He declares an ungodly man to be perfect while he is still ungodly. God places you before Him as though you had never committed a sin.

As Paul says, "Who shall lay anything to the charge of God's elect? It is God that justifieth" (Romans 8:33). Your sins have been forgiven. God has buried them in the depths of the sea and placed them behind His back of forgetfulness. Every sin is completely wiped out. You stand before God as a debtor, and you have received your discharge, you have become reconciled to God. You were actually an enemy of God before. The Bible says, "And all things are of God, who hath reconciled us to himself by Jesus Christ, and hath given to us the ministry of reconciliation" (2 Corinthians 5:18).

But more than all of that, you have been adopted into the family of God. You are now a child of God. "Having predestinated us unto the adoption of children by Jesus Christ to himself, according to the good pleasure of his will" (Ephesians 1:5). You are now a member of the royal family of heaven. You have royal blood in your veins. You are a child of the King. Even your friends will begin to notice the change that has taken place in your life. You have now been born again.

The Old and the New

Certain changes will take place once you have been born again. First, there will be a different attitude toward sin. You will learn to hate sin as God hates it. You will detest it and abhor it.

Down in Houston, Texas, a man was born again in one of our meetings. He owned a liquor store. The next morning he had a sign on the front of his door saying, "Out of business."

I heard about a man some time ago who had been born again in an evangelistic service. He was known as the city drunk. He was called "Old John." Somebody spoke to him the next morning on the street and said, "Good morning, Old John."

He said, "Who are you talking to? My name is not Old John. I'm *new* John." A complete revolution had taken place in his life.

Second, you will know that you have been born again because you will want to obey God. "And hereby we do know that we know him, if we keep his commandments" (1 John 2:3).

Third, you will be separated from the world. The Bible says, "Love not the world, neither the things that are in the world. If any man love the world, the love of the Father is not in him" (1 John 2:15). An unknown poet explains it this way:

All the water in the world,
However hard it tried,
Could never sink a ship
Unless it got inside.
All the evil in the world,
The wickedness and sin,
Could never sink the soul's craft
Unless it got inside.

Fourth, there will be a new love in your heart for other people. The Bible says, "We know that we have passed from death unto life, because we love the brethren" (1 John 3:14).

Fifth, we will not practice sin. The Bible says, "We know that whosoever is born of God sinneth not" (1 John 5:18). We will not engage in sinful practices.

In Texas they tell a story about a man who used to hitch his horse every morning in front of the saloon. One morning the saloonkeeper came out and found that the horse was hitched in front of the Methodist Church. He saw the man walking down the street and called out, "Say, why is your horse hitched in front of the Methodist Church this morning?"

The man turned around and said, "Well, last night I was converted in the revival meeting, and I've changed hitching posts."

That's what it means to be born again. That's what it means to be converted. That's what it means to be separated from the world. It means that you change hitching posts.

13

How to Be Sure

> *These things have I written unto you that believe on the name of the Son of God; that ye may know that ye have eternal life, and that ye may believe on the name of the Son of God.*
>
> 1 John 5:13

EVERY week I receive scores of letters from those who say they have doubts and uncertainties concerning the Christian life. Many come from genuine Christians who seem to have none of the joy of Christian faith, or the assurance, because they have failed to understand a basic truth of Christian experience. Even though the Bible says, "But these [the Bible] are written that ye might believe that Jesus is the Christ, the Son of God; and that believing ye might have life through his name" (John 20:31), many are unsure.

Now let's use this chapter to sum up what has happened to us. We have seen what it means to repent, to have faith, and to be born again. Now, how can I be certain, how can I be sure that all of this has happened to me? Many people with whom I talk have repented and have believed and have been born again, but they often lack the assurance of their conversion. Let's go over a few things that we've learned. First of all, becoming a Christian can be a crisis experience in your life, or it can be a process with a climactic moment of which you may or may not be conscious. Do not misunderstand me; you do not become a Christian as a result of a process of education. Some years ago a great preacher said, "We must so educate and train our youth in the Christian way of life that they will never know when they were not Christians." Much of the philosophy of religious education has been based upon this premise, and perhaps many have missed the essence of Christian experience because nothing more than religious training took its place. No change took place in the heart.

At the turn of the century, Professor Starbuck, a leading thinker in the field of psychology, observed that Christian workers generally were recruited from the ranks of those who had had a vital experience of conversion. He also observed that those who had a clear concept of what it means to be converted were mainly those who had come out of rural areas where in the early days they had had either little or no carefully planned religious training.

This is not a criticism of religious training, but it may be taken as a warning of the dangers involved in improper use of religious training that becomes a substitute for the experience of the new birth.

Religion Is Not Rebirth

To Nicodemus, one of the most religious men of his times, Jesus said, "Except a man be born again, he cannot see the kingdom of God" (John 3:3). Nicodemus could not substitute his profound knowledge of religion for spiritual rebirth, and we have not progressed beyond this point in our generation.

The ugly larva in its cocoon spends much time in almost unnoticeable growth and change. But no matter how slow that growth may be, the moment comes when it passes through a crisis and emerges a beautiful butterfly. The weeks of silent growth are important, but they cannot take the place of that experience when the old and the ugly are left behind and the new and the beautiful come into being.

It is true that thousands of Christians do not know the exact day or hour that they came to know Christ. Their faith and lives testify that consciously or unconsciously they have been converted to Christ. Whether they can remember it or not, there was a moment when they did cross over the line from death to life.

Probably everyone has had doubts and uncertainties at times in his religious experience. When Moses went up on Mount Sinai to receive the tables of the law from the hand of God, he was lost for some time to the sight of the Hebrews who stood anxiously waiting his return. They finally became doubtful and said among themselves, "As for this Moses, the man that brought us up out of the land of Egypt, we wot not what is become of him" (Exodus 32:1). Their defection was a result of their doubting and uncertainty.

The dreadful uncertainty that haunts the souls of multitudes grows out of a misunderstanding of what constitutes true Christian experience. Many do not seem to understand the nature of Christian experience, while others have been misinformed and are seeking something for which we are not warranted by Scripture to expect.

More than three hundred times the word *faith* is mentioned in the New Testament with reference to man's salvation, and many more times it is implied. The writer of the Book of Hebrews said, "He that cometh to God must believe that he is, and that he is a rewarder of them that diligently seek him." And again he said that "Without faith it is impossible to please him" (Hebrews 11:6).

It is because we have confused *faith* with *feeling* that many experience the difficulty and uncertainty that is so common among professing Christians today.

Faith always implies an object—that is, when we believe, we must believe something. That something I call the *fact*. Let me give you, then, three words, three words that must always be kept in the same order and never rearranged. Let me give you these three words that will point the way, for you, out of uncertainty to a confident Christian life. These three words are *fact*, *faith*, and *feeling*. They come in this order and the order is essential. If you confuse them, eliminate one, or add one, you will end up in the mire of despair and continue to grope about in semidarkness, without the joy and confidence of one who can say, "I know him in whom I have believed" (2 Timothy 1:12).

Fact

If you are saved from sin at all, you are saved through a personal faith in the gospel of Christ as defined in the Scriptures. Though it may at first seem dogmatic and narrow to you, the fact remains that there is no other way. The Bible says, "I delivered unto you first of all that which I also received, how that Christ died for our sins according to the Scriptures; and that he was buried, and that he arose again the third day according to the Scriptures" (1 Corinthians 15:3, 4). The Bible says that we are saved when our faith is in this objective fact. The work of Christ is a fact, His cross is a fact, His tomb is a fact, and His resurrection is a fact.

It is impossible to believe anything into existence. The gospel did not come into being because men believed it. The tomb was not emptied of its deposit that first Easter because some faithful persons believed it. The fact always preceded the faith. We are psychologically incapable of believing without an object of our faith.

The Bible does not call upon you to believe something that is not credible, but to believe in the fact of history that in reality transcends all history. The Bible calls upon you to believe that this work of Christ, done for sin and for sinners, is effective in all who will risk their souls with Him. Trusting in Him for your eternal salvation is trusting in a fact.

Faith

Faith is second in this order of three words. Faith is rationally impossible where there is nothing to believe. Faith must have an object. The object of Christian faith is Christ. Faith means more than an intellectual assent to the claims of Christ. Faith involves the will. It is volitional. Faith demands action. If we actually believe, then we will live. Faith without works is dead. Faith actually means surrender and commitment to the claims of Christ. It means an acknowledgment of sin and a turning to Christ. We do not know Christ through the five physical senses, but we know Him through the sixth sense that God has given every man—which is the ability to believe.

The Experience of Faith

In reading carefully through the New Testament to see just what kind of an experience you can expect, I find that the New Testament sets forth only one. There is just one experience for which you can look—only one feeling you can expect—and that is the experience of faith. Believing is an experience as real as any experience, yet many are looking for something more—some dramatic sensation that will bring a physical thrill, while others look for some spectacular manifestation. Many have been told to look for such sensations, but the Bible says that a man is "justified by faith" and not by feeling. A man is saved by trusting in the finished work of Christ on the cross and not by physical excitement or religious ecstasy.

But you may say to me, "What about feeling? Is there no place in saving faith for any feeling?" Certainly there is room for feeling in saving faith, but we are not saved by it. Whatever feeling there may be is only the result of saving faith, but it in itself is not what does the saving!

Feeling

Feeling is the last of the three words and is the least important. I believe that much religious unrest and uncertainty is caused by earnest, honest seekers after salvation who have a pre-determined idea that they must be in some kind of an emotional state before they can experience conversion.

Those who are seeking salvation as it is presented through the Scriptures will want to know what kind of an experience the Bible leads you to expect. I speak to those who have gone often to an altar, or to an inquiry room, or perhaps have knelt beside a radio or television set when an invitation has been given to receive Christ. You have heard the message, you have known that you were a sinner in need of the Savior, you have recognized that your life is a spiritual wreck, you have tried every man-made scheme for self-improvement and for reformation, but they all failed. In your lost and hopeless condition you looked to Christ for salvation. You believed that He could and would save you. You have often read His invitation to sinners when He said, "Come unto me, all ye that labor and are heavy laden, and I will give you rest" (Matthew 11:28). You have read the promise that says, "Him that cometh unto me, I will in no wise cast out" (John 6:37). You have read how He said, "If any man thirst, let him come unto me and drink" (John 7:37).

Feeling Comes After Faith

When I understand something of Christ's love for me as a sinner, I respond with a love for Christ—and love has feeling.

But love for Christ is a love that is above human love, though there is a similarity. It is a love that frees us from self. In marriage there is commitment. There is also feeling. But feelings come and go. Commitment stays. We who have committed ourselves to Christ have feelings that come and go—joy, love, gratitude, and so on. But the commitment remains unchanged. Feelings are important but not essential. The Bible says, "Perfect love casteth out fear" (1 John 4:18). And those who love Christ have that confidence in Him that raises them above fear. Psychologists tell us there is destructive fear and healthy fear. Healthy fear is *instructive,* causing us to care for our bodies and our loved ones—Jesus told us to *fear* Satan.

When I understand that Christ in His death gained a decisive victory over death and over sin, then I lose the fear of death. The Bible says that "He also himself likewise took part of the same that through death he might destroy him that had the power of death, that is, the devil; And deliver them who through fear of death were all their lifetime subject to bondage" (Hebrews 2:14, 15). Surely this also is a feeling. Fear is a kind of feeling, and to overcome fear with boldness and confidence in the very face of death is feeling and experience. But again I say, it is not the feeling of boldness and confidence that saves us, but it is our faith that saves us, and boldness and confidence result from our having trusted in Christ. From Genesis to Revelation we are told to fear the Lord. It is the fear of the Lord that puts all other fears in proper perspective.

The Part Guilt Plays

To have a guilty conscience is an experience. Psychologists may define it as a guilt experience and may seek to rationalize away the sense of guilt; but once this has been awakened through the application of the law of God, no explanation will quiet the insistent voice of conscience. Many a criminal has finally given himself over to the authorities because the accusations of a guilty conscience were worse than prison bars.

In an article on guilt which appeared in *The New York Times* (29 November 1983) Dr. Helen Block Lewis, a psychoanalyst and psychologist at Yale University, described guilt as a feeling that "helps people stay connected" to their fellow human beings.

"Guilt is one of the cements that binds us together and keeps us human," she explained. "If it occurs to you that you've done something to injure someone else, guilt compels you to do something to fix it, to repair the bond."

Samuel Rutherford said to "Pray for a strong and lively sense of sin; the greater the sense of sin, the less sin." A sense of sin and guilt is the same thing. It not only tells you when you are in trouble, but like the sense of pain it can keep you out of it. Without a sense of pain one could put his hand on a hot stove and feel nothing. The vital part that a sense of pain plays in keeping us healthy is explored in the book, *Fearfully and Wonderfully Made,* by Paul Brand and Philip Yancey. They explain that it is not the disease of leprosy itself which causes the deformation so common among lepers. It is the absence of a sense of pain when the extremities are injured (for instance, the hand in a fire) which causes the horrible mutilation associated with leprosy.

The Bible teaches that Christ cleanses the conscience. The Bible says, "For if the blood of bulls and of goats and the ashes of an heifer sprinkling the unclean sanctifieth to the purifying of the flesh: How much more shall the blood of Christ, who through the eternal Spirit offered himself without spot to God, purge your conscience from dead works to serve the living God?" (Hebrews 9:13, 14).

To have a guilty conscience cleansed, and to be free from its constant accusation is an experience, but it is not the cleansing of the conscience that saves you; it is faith in Christ that saves, and a cleansed conscience is the *result* of having come into a right relationship with God.

Joy is a feeling. Inward peace is a feeling. Love for others is a feeling. Concern for the lost is a feeling.

Finally, someone may say, "I believe the historic facts of

the gospel, but still I am not saved." Perhaps so, for the faith that saves has one distinguishing quality—saving faith is a faith that produces obedience, it is a faith that brings about a way of life. Some have quite successfully imitated this way of life for a time, but for those who trust Christ for salvation, that faith brings about in them a desire to live out that inward experience of faith. It is a power that results in godly living and surrender.

Let that intellectual faith, that historical faith that you may now have, yield itself to Christ in full surrender, earnestly desiring His salvation, and upon the authority of the Word of God you will become a child of God. "But as many as received him, to them gave he the right to become the sons of God, even to them that believe on his name" (John 1:12).

PART THREE

Applying the Antidote

14

Enemies of the Christian

For we wrestle not against flesh and blood, but against principalities, against powers, against the rulers of darkness of this world, against spiritual wickedness in high places.

Ephesians 6:12

NOW that you have made your decision—now that you have been born again—now that you have been converted—now that you have been justified—now that you are a child of God—what next? Is that all there is to it? Just one moment of decision and then it is all over? "Do I have any more responsibilities?" you ask.

Ah, yes, you have just begun the Christian life. You have just been born into a new world—the spiritual world. Everything is brand new. You are actually a spiritual baby. You need tenderness, love, care, nurture. You need to be fed. You need protection. That is one of the reasons why Christ established the church. It is nearly impossible to live the Christian life alone. Most of us need help and fellowship.

The newborn Christian is like a newborn baby in his need for love. While revising this book, my wife and I took an island vacation with our oldest daughter, her husband, and their seventh child, little three-month-old Anthony—our sixteenth grandchild. In the week we were together he cried only twice. Why? He was surrounded by tenderness, love, care, nurture. All he did was eat, sleep, and smile. Ideally, at the outset of their spiritual experience, "baby" Christians need this kind of nurture, but unfortunately our world is not geared to that kind of beginning for the Christian life. The church is the place where that beginning takes place, in the plan and purpose of God.

Possibly you have already found that you have enemies. These are dangerous, vicious enemies who will use any method to defeat you in your Christian life. Within minutes after you made your decision you found these enemies already at work: either you were tempted to commit some sin, or you had a moment of depression and discouragement. To be sure, everything is exciting and thrilling just after you have made your decision for Christ! But it is also natural to have doubts, problems, questions, temptations, discouragements, and even difficulties.

The Bible teaches that you have three enemies which will be warring against you as long as you live. You must be prepared. They must be warded off.

First, let's look at these enemies whom we must face. Let's unmask them and see what they are, and who they are, and how they operate.

The Devil

First—*the devil.* We have already seen that the devil is a mighty being who opposes God and tempts God's people. We have found that even though he was beaten at the cross by Christ he still has power to influence men for evil. The Bible calls him "the wicked one," "the devil," "a murderer," "a liar, and the father of lies," "an adversary" who seeks to devour, "that old serpent," and "accuser of our brethren" (Matthew 13:19; Luke 4:33; John 8:44; 1 Peter 5:8; Revelation 12:9–10).

The moment you made your decision for Christ, Satan suffered a tremendous defeat. He is angry now. From now on he is going to tempt you and try to lead you into sin. Don't be alarmed. He cannot rob you of your salvation, and he need not rob you of your assurance and victory. He will do everything in his power to sow seeds of doubt in your mind as to whether your conversion is a reality or not. You cannot argue with him for he is the greatest debater of all time.

The moment of test has come with the first temptation. Remember to refuse any reliance upon your feelings; they will change like a weather vane in a whirlwind. His next approach probably will be to make you feel proud and important—to make you confident of your own powers, ambitions, desires, and aims. On another occasion he will put hatred in your heart. He will tempt you to say unkind and ungenerous things about others. He will put envy, discontent, and malice in your heart. Then on another occasion he will tempt you to lie, and you could easily find yourself being a hypocrite. Lying is one of the worst of all sins and can be committed by a thought, word, or deed. Anything that is intended to deceive another person is lying. The devil will do his best to make a liar of you. He also will try to get you to work for him to tempt others to sin—to try to lead other Christian friends astray. If you are not careful you will find yourself actually in the employ of the devil. He is powerful, slick, crafty, wily, and subtle. He is called the "god of this world," "the prince of this world," "the prince and power of the air" (2 Corinthians 4:4; John 12:31; Ephesians 2:2).

The devil will try to discourage you, to divert you; he will seek to dilute your testimony; he will attempt anything to destroy your relationship to Christ and your influence upon others.

You ask "How can I overcome him? What can I do? Which way can I turn? Is there any escape?"

"There hath no temptation taken you but such as is common to man: but God is faithful, who will not suffer you to be tempted above that ye are able; but will with the temptation also make a way to escape, that ye may be able to bear it" (1 Corinthians 10:13).

Years ago I heard my friend J. Edwin Orr compare the Christian attacked by Satan to a mouse being attacked by a housewife wielding a broom. The mouse does not sit there contemplating the housewife or the broom. He is busy looking for a hole—a way to escape. So we Christians under satanic attack should look for our "way of escape."

God says in this verse that He has made a way of escape. Now remember this: temptation of the devil is not a sign that your life is not right with God. It is actually a sign that you are right with God. Temptation is not sin. Also remember that God never tempts His own children. He never causes His children to doubt. All doubts and temptations come from the devil. Remember also that Satan can only tempt. He can never compel you to yield to the temptation. Remember also that Satan has already been conquered by Christ. His power is made inoperative in the life of a fully trusting and yielded Christian who is completely dependent upon God.

The poet put it this way:

> *The devil trembles when he sees*
> *the weakest saint upon his knees.*

To say that Satan will be defeated when we read or quote Scripture and will run like a scalded dog when we resist him is an oversimplification. But we can depend upon the blood of Christ when we are under attack. There are times when we simply must hide behind the Person of Christ and ask Him to handle our problems. Jude says, "Yet Michael the archangel, when contending with the devil he disputed about the body of Moses, durst not bring against him a railing accusation, but said, The Lord rebuke thee" (v. 9). That's what we need to do—call upon God.

Now the Bible says that we are to "resist the devil and he will flee" from us (James 4:7). But before that, God says "Submit yourselves . . . to God." If you have fully submitted, one hundred percent yielded and surrendered yourself to Christ, then you can "resist the devil," and the Bible promises he will flee from you. The devil will tremble when you pray. He will be defeated when you quote or read a passage of Scripture to him, and will leave you when you resist him.

The World

Your second enemy is *the world.* The world means the cosmos, this world system. The world has a tendency to lead us into sin—evil companions, pleasures, fashions, opinions, and aims.

You will find in your born-again experience that your pleasures have been lifted into an entirely new and glorious realm. Many non-Christians have accused the Christian life as being a set of rules, taboos, vetos, and prohibitions. This is another lie of the devil. It is not a series of "don'ts," but a series of "dos." You become so busy in the work of Christ and so completely satisfied with the things of Christ that you do not have time for the things of the world.

Suppose someone should offer me a hamburger after I had eaten a T-bone steak. I would say, "No, thank you, I am already satisfied."

Young Christian, that is the secret. You are so filled with the things of Christ, so enamored of the things of God, that you do not have time or taste for sinful pleasures of this world. The Bible says, "The full soul loatheth an honey-comb; but to the hungry soul every bitter thing is sweet" (Proverbs 27:7).

Worldliness, however, has been vastly misunderstood on the part of thousands of Christians. It needs a little clarification. It is probably one of the greatest difficulties that meets a young and inexperienced Christian.

Dr. W. H. Griffith Thomas has said, "There are certain elements of daily life which are not sinful in themselves, but which have a tendency to lead to sin if they are abused. Abuse literally means extreme use, and in many instances overuse of things lawful becomes sin. Pleasure is lawful in use but unlawful in its overuse. Ambition is an essential part of true character, but it must be fixed on lawful objects and exercised in proper proportion. Our daily occupation, reading, dress, friendships and other similar phases of life are all legitimate and necessary, but can easily become ille-gitimate, unnecessary and harmful. Thought about the necessities of life is absolutely essential, but this can easily degenerate into anxiety, and then as Christ reminds us in the parable, the cares of this life choke the spiritual seed in the heart. Making of money is necessary for daily living, but money-making is apt to degenerate into money-loving and then the deceitfulness of riches enters into and spoils our spiritual life. Worldliness is thus not confined to any particular rank, walk, or circumstance of life so that we cannot separate this class from that and call one worldly and the other unworldly . . . one spiritual and the other unspiritual. Worldliness is a spirit, an atmosphere, an influence permeating the whole of life and human society, and it needs to be guarded against constantly and strenuously."

The Bible says, "Love not the world, neither the things that are in the world" (1 John 2:15). The Bible also warns that the world and the "lust thereof" shall pass away, "but he that doeth the will of God abideth forever" (1 John 2:17).

However, under certain conditions these can become perplexing problems in our modern-day living. Many young people come to me and ask, "Is this wrong?" or "Is that wrong?" "Is this sinful?" or "Is that sinful?" One simple question, earnestly and prayerfully asked, will settle about ninety percent of your problems along this line. Just ask this question to yourself every time: "What would Christ have me to do?" Another question you can ask is, "Can I ask His blessing upon this particular thing for me?" "What would Christ think about my amusements, recreation, books, companions, and television programs?" "Could I ask Christ to go along with me to this particular event?" Being omnipotent, He'll be there anyway. The point is, should you?

It does not mean that in society we are snobs or have a superiority complex, lest we be in danger of spiritual pride—which would be far worse than any worldliness. But today there are so many professing Christians who are walking hand in hand with the world that you cannot tell the difference between the Christian and the unbeliever. This should never be.

The Christian should stand out like a sparkling diamond against a rough background. He should be more wholesome than anyone else. He should be poised, cultured, courteous, gracious, but firm in the things that he does and does not do. He should laugh and be radiant, but he should refuse to allow the world to pull him down to its level.

The Bible says that "whatsoever is not of faith is sin" (Romans 14:23), and the Bible again says that he who doubts is condemned if he does it. In other words, we are never to do anything of which we are not perfectly clear and certain. If you have a doubt about that particular thing that is bothering you, as to whether it is worldly or not, the best policy is "don't do it."

The Flesh

The third enemy that you will face immediately is *the lust of the flesh*. The flesh is that evil tendency of your inward self. Even after you are converted, sometimes your old, sinful cravings will return. You become startled and wonder where they come from. The Bible teaches that the old nature, with all its corruption, is still there and that these evil temptations come from nowhere else. In other words, "a traitor is living within." "That wretched bent toward sin is ever present to drag you down." War has been declared! You now have two natures in conflict, and each one is striving for dominance.

The Bible teaches "the flesh lusteth against the Spirit, and the Spirit against the flesh" (Galatians 5:17). It is the battle of the self-life and the Christ-life. This old nature cannot please God. It cannot be converted, or even patched up. Thank God, when Jesus died He took you with Him, and the old nature can be made inoperative and you can "reckon ye also yourselves to be dead indeed unto sin" (Romans 6:11). This is done by faith.

However, you must distinguish very carefully again between use and abuse—between that which is lawful and that which is unlawful. Some of these things that will be cropping up may be sinful lusts, or they may not be.

As Dr. W. H. Griffith Thomas says, "The original meaning of the word lust is 'strong desire' and not necessarily a sinful desire, since there are certain desires of our physical nature—such as hunger and thirst—which we have in common with the animal world and which, in themselves, are natural and not sinful. It is only their abuse that is evil. Hunger is a natural lust. Gluttony is a sinful lust. Thirst is a natural lust. Intemperance is a sinful lust. Sloth should not be confused with exhaustion or illness. Marriage is according to the will of God and the dictates of human nature, physical, mental and social. Adultery is a sin and is opposed to the will of God and to all that is pure in body, mind and heart. But there are other lusts of the flesh which are sensually and inherently sinful. Such as, for instance, the desire to gratify at all cost our hatred and revenge. We must, therefore, distinguish carefully between the lust which is simply a strong desire, and the same lust as a sinful desire. Sins of the flesh are in some respects the most terrible of all because they represent the yearnings of the nature to do evil. Neither the devil nor the world, nor even our own evil heart can compel us to sin. It must be by our consent and will and it is at this point that our evil nature comes in with its awful power and possibility of evil."

Paul said he had no confidence in the flesh. On another occasion he said, "I make no provision for the flesh" (Romans 13:14). On another occasion he said, "I keep my body under" (1 Corinthians 9:27). We are so to re-yield and re-surrender ourselves to God that we can, by faith, reckon the old nature dead indeed unto sin.

Fighting Our Foes

These then, are our three foes: the devil, the world, and the flesh. Our attitude toward them as Christians can be summed up in one word—*renounce.* There can be no bargaining, compromise, or hesitation. Abiding in Christ, as taught in John 15, is the only possible course for the Christian who has to be "in" the world but does not want to be "of" it. Someone has said that the apostle Paul was dealing with this dilemma when he wrote to the Ephesians, "Paul, an apostle of Jesus Christ . . . to the saints . . . at Ephesus and to the faithful in Christ Jesus" (Ephesians 1:1). Ephesus was their business address, but "in Christ" was their home address! In relation to the devil, we resist him only as we submit ourselves to God. In relation to the world, the Bible says, "This is the victory that overcometh the world, even our faith" (1 John 5:4). In relation to the flesh, the Bible says, "Walk in the Spirit, and ye shall not fulfill the lust of the flesh" (Galatians 5:16).

Here is glorious news to you who have already been fighting these battles and temptations. You are not asked to fight the battle alone. The Bible says in Romans 8:13 that you, *by the Spirit,* shall put to death the deeds of the body.

Remember, Jesus promised that He would never leave us or forsake us. Remember, Jesus promised us that after He left the earth He would send Another—the Third Person of the Trinity—the Holy Spirit, who is called a Comforter (which actually means "one who comes alongside to help"), that He may abide with us forever (John 14:16). Jesus said, "I am not going to leave you alone. I will come to you in the person of the Holy Spirit." Jesus is the vine and believers are the branches is the way Jesus put it (see John 15).

The Holy Spirit is the most powerful Being in the world today. The time of the Old Testament was an age of God the Father. During the time that Jesus was on earth it was an age of God the Son. Now we are living, since Pentecost, in the age of God the Holy Spirit. The Bible says, "Be filled with the Spirit" (Ephesians 5:18), which reads literally, "Be *being* filled . . . ." It's a continuous and ongoing process. Just as Christ came to make God visible and redeem mankind, so the Holy Spirit came to make Christ visible in the life of the believer and enable the individual Christian to offer Christ's redemption to a lost and dying world.

The Bible says that the moment you accepted Christ as Savior the Holy Spirit took up residence in your heart. Your body is now "the temple of the Holy Ghost *which is in you*" (1 Corinthians 6:19). Paul even warned that if any man has not the Spirit of Christ he is none of His.

You say, "But I don't feel anything down in my heart. I don't feel the Spirit of God in me."

Faith Is a Fact

Disregard feelings. You're not saved by feeling, and you may or may not feel the Spirit. Accept Him by faith as a fact. He lives within you right now to help you live the

Christian life. He is living in you in order to magnify, glorify, and exalt Christ in you so that you can live a happy, victorious, radiant, Christ-honoring life.

The Bible commands, "Be filled with the Spirit" (Ephesians 5:18). If you are filled with the Spirit, then you are going to produce the fruit of the Spirit, which is "love, joy, peace, longsuffering, gentleness, goodness, faith, meekness, temperance" (Galatians 5:22–23). To be filled with the Spirit is not optional. It is a command to be obeyed—a duty to be done.

How do you know that you are filled? And how can you be filled? Is it some emotional experience through which you must pass? Not necessarily. When you give all you know of yourself to all that you know of Him, then you can accept by faith that you are filled with the Spirit of God. That means that He can have all of you. Commitment actually is surrender—total, absolute, unconditional, irreversible surrender. "I beseech you, therefore, brethren, by the mercies of God, that ye present your bodies a living sacrifice, holy, acceptable unto God, which is your reasonable service" (Romans 12:1).

It is only the consecrated, Spirit-filled Christian who can have victory over the world, the flesh, and the devil. It is the Holy Spirit who will do the fighting for you. "We wrestle not against flesh and blood, but against principalities, against powers, against the rulers of darkness" (Ephesians 6:12). This is a spiritual warfare. You cannot fight against these three enemies with normal weapons. Only as we become channels and let the Holy Spirit do the fighting through us are we going to get complete victory. Don't hold back anything from Christ. Let Him be completely the Lord and Master of your life. He said, "Ye call me Master and Lord: and ye say well; for so I am" (John 13:13).

I believe unself-consciousness is characteristic of the fruit of the Holy Spirit. The person who says, "I am Spirit-filled" sets himself up for some pretty uncomfortable scrutiny. Did any apostle or disciple say of himself, "I am filled with the Holy Spirit"? But of many it was said, "They were filled with the Holy Spirit." The person who is self-consciously loving, self-consciously joyful, self-consciously peaceful, has about him the odor of self. And as one Christian sanely observed, "Self is spiritual B.O."

A little child playing one day with a very valuable vase put his hand into it and could not withdraw it. His father, too, tried his best, but all in vain. They were thinking of breaking the vase when the father said, "Now, my son, make one more try. Open your hand and hold your fingers out straight as you see me doing, and then pull."

To their astonishment the little fellow said, "O no, father. I couldn't put my fingers out like that, because if I did I would drop my penny."

Smile, if you will—but thousands of us are like that little boy, so busy holding on to the world's worthless penny that we cannot accept liberation. I beg you to drop that trifle in your heart. Surrender! Let go, and let God have His way in your life.

Now, after you have given yourself completely to Christ in consecration, remember that God has accepted what you have presented. "Him that cometh unto me I will in no wise cast out" (John 6:37). You have come to Him; now He has received you. And He will in no wise cast you out!

The Fruit of the Spirit

Not only will you have boldness, but you will produce the fruit of the Spirit. Keep in mind that these fruits of the Spirit are *of* the Spirit. One does not produce them himself. They are supernatural in origin. The first is, according to Galatians 5, love, and from this root will grow all the others. Jesus said, "This is my commandment, that ye love one another, as I have loved you. . . . If ye keep my commandments ye shall abide in my love; even as I have kept my Father's commandments, and abide in his love" (John 15:12, 10). We must differentiate between the *gifts* of the Spirit and the *fruit* of the Spirit. Gifts are *given*— fruits are *grown*. To grow something there must be a close, intimate, personal relationship between the vine and the branch. A person must be rooted and grounded in Christ.

As we pointed out earlier, one of the characteristics of the Holy Spirit is unself-consciousness. Whenever a person is self-conscious of spiritual fruit there goes up the odor of self.

Another fruit of the Spirit is joy. One of the characteristics of the Christian is an inward joy that does not depend upon circumstances. Nehemiah says, "For the joy of the Lord is your strength" (8:10). S. D. Gordon, the well-known devotional writer of a past generation, said of joy: "Joy is distinctly a Christian word and a Christian thing. It is the reverse of happiness. Happiness is the result of what happens of an agreeable sort. Joy has its springs deep down inside. And that spring never runs dry, no matter what happens. Only Jesus gives that joy. He had joy, singing its music within, even under the shadow of the cross. It is an unknown word and thing except as He has sway within."

"Real joy comes not from ease or riches or . . . the praise

of men, but from doing something worthwhile," said the missionary Sir Wilfred Grenfell. And Alexander MacLaren said, "To pursue joy is to lose it. The only way to get it is to follow steadily the path of duty, without thinking of joy, and then, like sheep, it comes most surely, unsought, and we 'being in the way' the angel of God, fair-haired joy, is sure to meet us."

There will be peace. Paul said, "Troubled on every side, yet not distressed; we are perplexed, but not in despair; persecuted, but not forsaken; cast down, but not destroyed" (2 Corinthians 4:8–9). We could go through all the rest of the supernatural list—longsuffering, gentleness, goodness, faith, meekness, and temperance—and see how all of this fruit flourishes in the lives of those who are truly yielded and Spirit-filled.

The victory is yours. Claim it! It is your birthright. Browning said, "The best is yet to be." This doesn't mean the Christian can never suffer defeat or experience low periods in life. But it does mean that the Savior goes with you no matter the problem. The peace comes in the midst of problems and in spite of them.

15

Guidelines for Christian Living

And as ye would that men should do to you,
do ye also to them likewise.

Luke 6:31

WHETHER we are playing a game, driving a car, or baking a cake, there are certain rules that must be followed for our safety as well as our success.

I well recall what happened near my home in Montreat, North Carolina, some years ago. The road between Black Mountain and Asheville was being widened from two lanes to four. For several weeks during the construction period there were no lane markers. One night there was a tragic head-on collision and five people were killed—because the "road rules" had not been clearly marked.

The Bible teaches that the Christian life is one of constant growth. When you were born again, you were born into God's family. My wife Ruth and I now have sixteen grandchildren. And each of them is precious to us. Each is an accepted, treasured member of our family. And that's the way God feels about you. It is God's purpose that you will grow into full stature and become mature in Christ. It would be against the law of God and nature if you were to remain a baby and thus become a spiritual dwarf. In 2 Peter 3:18, the Bible says that we are to grow. This implies steady development, constant enlargement, increasing wisdom.

Read the Bible Daily

For one to grow properly certain rules must be observed for good spiritual health. First: you should *read your Bible daily.* It is one of your greatest privileges. Your spiritual life needs food. What kind of food? Spiritual food. Where do you find this spiritual food? In the Bible, the Word of God. The Bible reveals Christ, who is the Bread of Life for your hungry soul, and the Water of Life for your thirsty heart. If you fail to partake of daily spiritual nourishment, you will starve and lose your spiritual vitality. The Bible says, "Desire the sincere milk of the Word, that ye may grow thereby" (1 Peter 2:2). Read it, study it, meditate on it, memorize it. Ninety-five percent of the difficulties you will experience as a Christian can be traced to a lack of Bible study and reading.

Suppose an archaeologist discovered the original diary of Genghis Khan, or Alexander the Great, or the love letters of Cleopatra? Or what if our astronauts had discovered a mysterious manuscript during their moon walk? Imagine the stampede into the bookstores across America to get copies of such books. Yet we have here a Book that God Himself has written for mankind—and think how it is either ignored or attacked by many so-called civilized people.

Some parts of our world do not enjoy the freedom we have to read the Bible and study it together with fellow

Christians. In most of the world, in fact, there's a veritable famine for the Word of God! I recall the story of a Chinese musician in the People's Republic of China. He was converted and strengthened spiritually through the reading of individual pages of the Scripture torn from a Bible and slipped to him by an unknown friend. There are other stories of prisoners who survived twenty to thirty years at hard labor—and sometimes terrible torture—and came out with their minds intact, totally lacking in bitterness toward their captors.

One more story of the Bible's power comes from a mental hospital here in this country. A young man, an inmate of the hospital, wrote to our organization requesting a copy of the Bible. His recovery and subsequent complete rehabilitation date back to his receipt of that Bible—and his reading of its pages. Today he is married and self-supporting!

Do not be content to skim through a chapter merely to satisfy your conscience. Hide the Word of God in your heart. A little portion well digested is of greater spiritual value to your soul than a lengthy portion scanned hurriedly. Do not be discouraged because you cannot understand it all. Some excuse themselves saying, "It's too hard to understand." Any book is difficult to understand if you don't read it! Read simple portions of the Bible first. You do not feed a baby beefsteak the first day—you give him milk.

I would suggest that you start by reading the Gospel of John. As you read, the Holy Spirit will enlighten the passages for you. He will illuminate the difficult words and make obscure meanings clear. Even though you cannot remember all you have read, or understand it all, go on reading. The very practice of reading in itself will have a purifying effect upon your mind and heart. Let nothing take the place of this daily exercise.

Scripture memorized can come to mind when you do not have your Bible with you—on sleepless nights, when driving a car, traveling, when having to make an instantaneous important decision. It comforts, guides, corrects, encourages—all we need is there. Memorize as much as you can.

Learn to Pray

Second: *learn the secret of prayer.* Your prayers may falter at first. You may be awkward and inarticulate. But the Holy Spirit who lives within you will help you and teach you. Every prayer that you pray will be answered. Sometimes the answer may be "Yes" and sometimes "No," and sometimes it is "Wait," but nevertheless it will be answered.

Prayer is communicating. A baby's first response is to his parents. He isn't asking for anything. He is simply smiling back when his parents smile, cooing when they talk to him. What a thrill his first response brings to the entire family! In the same way, can you imagine the joy our first response to Him brings to God?

Your petitions should always be conditioned by "Thy will be done." "Delight thyself also in the Lord and he shall give thee the desires of thine heart" (Psalm 37:4). But the delighting of oneself in Him precedes the fulfillment of our desires. Delighting ourselves in Him will direct our desires, so God *can answer* our petitions.

Remember that you can pray any time, anywhere. Washing dishes, digging ditches, working in the office, in the shop, on the athletic field even in prison—you can pray and know God hears! We have a friend on Death Row who prays for us every morning between four and six. How often this fact has encouraged and cheered us on.

Try to have a systematic method of prayer. Prayer combined with Bible study makes for a healthy Christian life. The Bible says, "Pray without ceasing." If you have special prayer periods that you set aside during the day, your unconscious life will be saturated with prayer between the prayer periods. It is not enough for you to get out of bed in the morning and just bow your knee and repeat a few sentences. There should be stated periods in which you slip apart with God. For the overworked mother or one living under extremely busy circumstances, this may be impossible. But here is where "prayer without ceasing" comes in. We pray as we work. As we have said, we pray everywhere, any time.

The devil will fight you every step of the way. He will cause the baby to cry, the telephone to ring, someone to knock at the door—there will be many interruptions, but keep at it! Don't be discouraged. Soon you will find that these periods of prayer are the greatest delight of your life. You will look forward to them with more anticipation than to anything else. Without constant, daily, systematic prayer your life will seem barren, discouraging, and fruitless. Without constant prayer you never can know the inner peace that God wants to give you.

Rely on the Holy Spirit

Third: *rely constantly on the Holy Spirit.* Remember that Christ dwells in you through the Holy Spirit. Your body is now the dwelling place of the Third Person of the Trinity. Do not ask Him to help you as you would a servant. Ask Him to come in and do it all. Ask Him to take over in your life.

Tell Him how weak, helpless, unstable, and unreliable you are. Stand aside and let Him take over in all the choices and decisions of your life. We know that the Holy Spirit prays for us (Romans 8), and what a comfort that should be to the weakest of us.

It is impossible for you to hold out in your Christian life—but He can hold you. It is very difficult for Him to hold you if you are struggling, fighting, and striving. Just relax and rest in the Lord. Let go all those inner tensions and complexes. Rely completely on Him. Do not fret and worry about important decisions—let Him make them for you. Do not worry about tomorrow—He is the God of tomorrow, He sees the end from the beginning. Do not worry about the necessities of life—He is there to supply and provide. A true victorious Christian is one who, in spite of worries, inner conflicts, and tensions, is confident that God is in control and will be victorious in the end. In reliance on the Holy Spirit, you will find that many of your physical and mental ailments will disappear along with many worries, inner conflicts, and tensions. Whatever our difficulties, whatever our circumstances, we must remember, as Corrie ten Boom used to say, "Jesus is victor!"

Attend Church Regularly

Fourth: *attend church regularly*. Christianity is a religion of fellowship. Following Christ means love, righteousness, service; and these can only be achieved and expressed through social relations. These social relationships are to be found in the church.

There is a visible church and there is an invisible

church. The invisible church is made up of true believers down through the centuries and the world over. The visible church is made up of both Catholic and Protestant—the latter with its various denominations. But we are told in the Scriptures, "Forsaking [not] the assembling of ourselves together . . ." (Hebrews 10:25). Christians need fellowship—the fellowship of fellow believers.

The visible church is Christ's organization upon earth. It is a place where we gather to worship God, learn from His Word, and fellowship with other Christians. The Bible calls the church "a holy nation," "God's own people," "the household of God," "a holy temple in the Lord," "a dwelling place of God in the Spirit," "the body of Christ." These are all figures of speech, symbols, or pictures used to indicate the spiritual reality of the church.

Nothing can take the place of church attendance. If you are a true follower of Christ you will scorn such flimsy excuses as the weather being too hot or too cold, rain or snow, as unworthy of a true follower of Christ. There are many people who say they can stay at home on Sunday morning and worship God in their own minds. The person who does only this fails to give God the complete worship to which He has a right, for God is the Creator of our bodies, no less than of our minds and souls; therefore both the mind and the body should participate in rendering to God a complete act of worship.

In certain countries today, however, church gatherings are not encouraged. For years people have been forced to meet privately in homes, perhaps just a single family or perhaps a few Christian friends gathering together. In the People's Republic of China the government has reopened some of the old churches. The packed buildings prove that what I have said above is true. Christians need one another; we need to gather together to worship God, and nothing can take the place of church attendance.

At the same time I think we should be grateful for the electronic church. There are many in hospitals, institutions, like old people's homes, or even prisons where the only way they have to attend a church service is by television or even radio.

On the other hand, there are many who claim they can stay at home and listen to a sermon on the radio or television and that this takes the place of a church service. That is not enough. You do not go to church to hear a sermon. You go to church to worship God and to serve Him in the fellowship of other Christians. You cannot be a successful and happy Christian without being faithful in church. In the church you will find your place of service. We are saved to serve. The happy Christian is the serving Christian.

Be a Witnessing Christian

Fifth: *be a witnessing Christian.* If you are faithfully practicing the four preceding rules this one will take care of itself—just as it follows naturally that if a cup is being filled continually it is bound to overflow.

Sometime ago I came across the question, which is more important, to witness by one's life or to witness by the Word? And the answer was, "Which is more important, the left or right wing of an airplane?" Thinking this very clever, I repeated it one day in a car as I was driving some missionaries out to lunch. One of them spoke up and said, "That's very clever. But it's just not true." Surprised, I asked what she meant. "All the way through the Scriptures," she replied,

"God has promised to bless His Word, not our lives: 'My Word shall not return unto me void but shall accomplish . . . He that hath my word let him preach my word faithfully, for what are the tares to the wheat, saith the Lord.'" I realized she was speaking the truth. We are responsible to God for the way in which we live, but it is His Word that He has promised to bless and this explains why a musician in a communist country can pick up a page torn from the Bible and be converted. That is why a surgeon general in Portugal, returning home on a muddy day and finding a piece of paper stuck to his shoe, can pull it off and read a portion of the Word of God and be converted.

We Christians are now duly appointed and commissioned ambassadors of the King of kings. We are to let our flag fly high over our embassy. Suppose our ambassador to Russia should order the American flag pulled down because it is not popular in Russia—we would soon call him home! He would not deserve to represent the United States.

If we are not willing to let our flags fly in the home, in the office, in the shop, on the campus—then we are not worthy to be ambassadors for Christ! We are to take our stand and let all those around us know that we are Christians. We are to bear witness for Christ.

We witness in two ways: by life and by word—and the two, where possible, should go hand in hand. God's purpose for you and me after we have been converted is that we be witnesses to His saving grace and power. We are to be commandos for Christ. We are to be minute-men for Him.

Christ said, "Whoever therefore shall confess me before men, him will I confess also before my Father which is in heaven" (Matthew 10:32). Acts 28:23 presents a thrilling scene. Paul, held in bonds at Rome, persuaded men concerning Jesus, from morning to evening. Concerning each of us it should be said every day, "Behold a sower went forth to sow."

Very little originality is permitted a Western Union messenger boy. His sole obligation is to carry the message he receives from the office to the person to whom it is addressed. He may not like to carry that message. It may contain bad news or distressing news for the person to whom he carries it. He cannot stop on the way, open the envelope, and change the wording of the telegram. His duty is to take the message.

We Christians have the Word of God. Our Great Commander has said, "Go, and take this message to a dying world." Some are neglecting it. Some are tearing up the message and substituting one of their own. Some are taking out a part of it. Some are telling the people that the Lord does not mean what He says. Others are saying that He really did not write the message but that it was written by ordinary men who are mistaken about the meaning of it.

Let us remember that the apostle Paul exhorted the Christians centuries ago to teach only the Word. Remember we are sowing seed. Some indeed may fall on beaten paths and some among thorns, but it is our business to keep on sowing. We are not to stop sowing because some of the soil looks unpromising.

We are holding a light. We are to let it shine! Though it may seem but a twinkling candle in a world of blackness, it is our business to let it shine.

We are blowing a trumpet. In the din and noise of battle the sound of our little trumpet may seem to be lost, but we must keep sounding the alarm to those who are in danger.

We are kindling a fire. In this cold world full of hatred and selfishness our little blaze may seem to be unavailing, but we must keep our fire burning.

We are striking with a hammer. The blows may seem only to jar our hands as we strike, but we are to keep on hammering. Amy Carmichael of India once asked a stone-cutter which blow broke the stone. "The first one and the last," he replied, "and every one in between."

We have bread for a hungry world. The people may seem to be so busy feeding on other things that they will not accept the Bread of Life, but we must keep on giving it, offering it to the souls of men.

We have water for famishing people. We must keep standing and crying out, "Ho, every one that thirsteth, come ye to the waters." Sometimes they can't come and we must carry it to them.

We must persevere. We must never give up. Keep using the Word!

Jesus said that much of our seed will find good soil and spring up and bear fruit. We must be faithful witnesses. The most thrilling experience known to man is to win another to Jesus Christ. It has been my privilege to win others to a saving knowledge of Christ. I never cease to thrill at hearing of one who has listened, accepted Christ, and been transformed by His grace. This is worth more than all the money in all the world. There is no happiness, no experience, no romantic adventure comparable to the thrill of winning another person to Christ.

The Bible says, "He that winneth souls is wise" (Proverbs 11:30). "And they that be wise shall shine as the brightness of the firmament; and they that turn many to righteousness as the stars for ever and ever" (Daniel 12:3).

"Ye are the salt of the earth" (Matthew 5:13). Salt makes one thirsty. Does your life make others thirsty for the water of life?

Let Us Love

Sixth: *let love be the ruling principle of your life. Be ruled by love.* Jesus said to those who followed Him, "By this shall all men know that ye are my disciples, if ye have love one to another." In another part of the Bible we find the same thing stated: "Beloved, let us love one another, for love is of God; and every one that loveth is born of God, and knoweth God. He that loveth not knoweth not God, for God is love. In this was manifested the love of God toward us, because that God sent his only begotten Son into the world, that we might live through him. Herein is love, not that we loved God, but that he loved us, and sent his Son to be the propitiation for our sins" (1 John 4:7–10). Love does not necessarily imply approval of the one loved. If God had waited until He could approve of us before He sent His Son to redeem us, where would we be?

Of all the gifts God offers His children, love is the greatest. Of all the fruits of the Holy Spirit, love is the first.

The Bible declares that we who follow Christ should love one another as God loved us when He sent His Son to die on the cross. The Bible says that the moment we come to Christ He gives us supernatural love and that His love is shed abroad in our hearts by the Holy Spirit. The greatest demonstration of the fact that we are Christians is that we love one another. If we learn this secret of God early in our Christian experience, we will have gone a long way toward a mature, happy Christian life.

Be an Obedient Christian

Seventh: *be an obedient Christian.* Let Christ have first place in all the choices of your life. Make Him Lord and Master.

Learn How to Meet Temptation

Eighth: *learn how to meet temptation.* As we have already learned, temptation is natural. Temptation is not sin. It is *yielding* that is sin. God never brings temptation to us. He allows it to test us. It is the work of the devil. Recognize it as such. One way to meet temptation is to quote a verse of Scripture at the Tempter—he will always run, for he cannot stand the Word of God.

When Jesus was tempted in the wilderness, the only resource that He had was the Word of God. He said three times, "It is written."

Say to the devil, "Thus saith the Lord," and he will flee. At the same time let Christ through the Holy Spirit do the fighting for you. Be like the little girl who said, "Every time I hear the devil knock, I send Jesus to the door."

Everyone has temptations but some folks entertain them. They seem to enjoy being tempted. Chase a mouse with a broom and you will notice that he isn't eyeing the broom. He is looking for a hole. Get your eyes off the temptation and onto Christ!

I once asked an army officer which he would rather have on the field of battle—courage or obedience. He flashed right back, "Obedience!"

God would rather have your obedience than anything else. In order to be obedient you must know His commands. That is another reason for the necessity of studying and reading the Bible. The Bible is your compass and rule book. Obey what God tells you.

Be a Wholesome Christian

Ninth: *be a wholesome Christian.* It has been well said that "Some Christians are so heavenly minded they are no earthly good."

Certainly the Bible teaches separation from sin, but the Bible says nowhere that we are to be peculiar or unnatural. We are to be radiant. We should be chivalrous, courteous, clean of body, pure of mind, poised, and gracious. Silly flirtations, unhealthy gossip, shady conversations, suggestive amusements should be avoided like rattlesnakes. We should be neat in appearance, clean, attractive, and as much as possible in style, with good taste. Extremes should be avoided. Our lives and appearance should commend the gospel and make it attractive to others. As the late Dr. Barnhouse once said, "Men may not read the gospel in sealskin, or the gospel in morocco, or the gospel in cloth covers; but they can't get away from the gospel in shoe leather."

Live Above Your Circumstances

Tenth: *live above your circumstances.* God made you as you are! He placed you where you are! So you can best serve and glorify Him just as you are, where you are. Some people are always looking on the other side of the fence because they think the grass is greener. They spend so much time wishing things were different, and thinking up alibis for why they are not, that they overlook all the advantages and opportunities open to them right where they are.

Be as the apostle Paul when he said, "But none of these things move me" (Acts 20:24). Paul said he had learned how to abound and how to be abased. He had learned to be every inch a Christian even in prison. Don't let your circumstances get you down. Learn to live graciously within them, realizing the Lord Himself is with you.

These principles and suggestions may seem simple—but keep them—they work. I have seen them tested in the lives of thousands. I have tested them in my own life. Properly and faithfully kept, they will give you peace of soul, happiness, peace of mind, and pleasure, and you will have learned the secret of living life with satisfaction.

16

The Christian and the Church

In whom ye also are builded together for an habitation of God through the Spirit.

Ephesians 2:22

MAN is a social animal, gregarious by nature, and finds his greatest sense of security and satisfaction in the company of others who share his interests and attitudes. Of all the many groups into which humans have collected themselves, of all the many tribes, clans, organizations, and societies throughout history, none has been so powerful, so far-reaching, or more universal than the church.

In primitive times, men gathered together for mutual protection, and at a far later date they learned to join together for mutual benefit and pleasure. With more advanced civilization, secret societies came into being, to give their members a sense of belonging, a feeling of being "set apart" and therefore distinguished from nonmembers. Special oaths, rituals, and codes were established and given great significance.

Racial and national groups were established with membership restricted to those of similar place of origin, or with allegiance to a common flag. Country clubs, college fraternities, lodges, literary societies, political parties, military organizations—all of these, from the most select "gentlemen's club" to the high school "gang," represent man's need to find comfort and reassurance in the company of others who approve of his way of life, because their own way of life is similar.

Nowhere, however, has man found this comfort, this reassurance, this peace to the extent that he has found it in the church, for all other groups are obviously man-inspired. They draw artificial boundaries and set up only the illusion of protection; while the church provides a living, vibrant organism that draws its power from God Himself, instead of relying upon outside sources to give it meaning and vitality.

Origin of the Church

The word *church* is an English translation of the Greek word *ecclesia,* which means "the called-out ones," or an assembly of people. Although *church* soon became a distinctively Christian word, it has a pre-Christian history. Throughout the Greek world the word *church* was the designation of the regular assembly of the whole body of citizens in a free city-state. A group of the citizens would be called out by the herald for the discussion and decision of public business. This same word *church* was also the Hebrew equivalent in the Old Testament and is translated in English as "congregation" or "community" of Israel in which members were designated as the called-out people of God. Thus we find Stephen in the Book of Acts using it when he describes Moses as "he that was in the church in the wilderness" (Acts 7:38). In the first century, therefore, the word *church* would suggest to the Greek a self-governing, democratic society; to the Jew, a theocratic society whose members were the subjects of God.

The word *church* as applied to the Christian society was first used by Jesus Himself when He told Peter, "Upon this rock I will build my church, and the gates of hell shall not prevail against it" (Matthew 16:18). Thus Jesus Christ Himself founded the church. He is the great cornerstone upon which the church is built. He is the foundation of all Christian experience, and the church is founded upon Him. "For other foundation can no man lay than that is laid, which is Jesus Christ" (1 Corinthians 3:11). Jesus proclaimed Himself to be the founder of the church, the builder of the church, and the church belongs to Him and to Him alone. He has promised to live with, and in, all those who are members of His church. Here is not only an organization but an organism which is completely unlike anything else that the world has ever known: God Himself living with, and in, ordinary men and women who are members of His church.

Jesus Christ Its Head

The New Testament teaches that while there is actually only one universal church there can be any number of local churches formed into various denominations and societies or councils. These local churches and denominational groups may be divided along national and theological lines or according to the temperament of their members. However, the New Testament teaches that even though there may be many cleavages and divisions within the structure of the church, yet we have only "one Lord." As the hymn puts it, "The church's one foundation is Jesus Christ her Lord."

Jesus Christ is the head of this great universal church. From Him must spring all the activities and teachings of the church, for He is the fountainhead of all Christian experience.

In this day of electronics it is easy to draw a comparison with a far-flung communications system in which there is one central station toward which all light or sound waves converge and from which all connections are made. In a railroad system there is always one central office from which orders governing the operations of all trains originate. In the army, one commanding general issues orders to the many groups under his jurisdiction. His various subordinates may interpret his orders in slightly different ways, but his orders still remain the basis for their conduct.

In relation to the church, Jesus Christ stands in the position of the commanding general. It is upon His orders that the church has its existence. Its very power comes directly from Him, and it is up to every church group to follow His commands as closely as possible. Just as the commanding general expects to have his orders carried out faithfully, so does Jesus expect every branch of the church to abide by His teachings to the fullest.

The church has been widely criticized for many internal squabbles, much hair-splitting and apparent lack of unity. These, however, are superficial things; these are the conflicts that come from the slightly varying interpretations of the general's orders and in no way reflect upon the wisdom of the general or His absolute authority in issuing His orders!

Study the underlying beliefs of the various denominations and you will find that basically and historically they are almost identical. They may differ widely in ritual, they may seem to lock horns over theological technicalities; but fundamentally they all recognize Jesus Christ as God incarnate, who died upon the cross and rose again that man might have salvation—and that is the all-important fact to all humanity.

The Church—or Churches?

Now that you have accepted Christ as your Savior and put your trust and confidence in Him, you have already become a member of the great church invisible. You are a member of the household of faith. You are a part of the body of Christ. Now you are called upon to obey Christ, and if you obey Christ, you will follow His example of joining with others in the worship of God. "Not forsaking the assembling of ourselves together, as the manner of some is" (Hebrews 10:25).

It is true that we are now talking about the local church, the one in your own community, of whose many imperfections and shortcomings you may be well aware. But we must remember that perfection does not exist among human beings, and the institutions they create to the greater glory of God are filled with these self-same flaws. Jesus is the only perfect Man who ever lived. The rest of us are at best but repentant sinners, try as we may to follow His magnificent example; and the church is but turning a blind eye toward itself when it claims infallibility or perfection for itself or any of its members.

Samuel Rutherford at one point received a complaint

from some church members who were unhappy with their pastor and the local church situation. He wrote them a very stern reply, telling them that they were not responsible for the life of their pastor. But they were responsible to pray for him, and to remain in the church, and to work for the Lord. And that the Lord would honor and bless them for it.

The Tabernacle under Eli had degenerated so terribly that the people despised the sacrifice of the Lord because Eli's "sons made themselves vile, and he restrained them not" (1 Samuel 3:13). But little Samuel was left in that environment and grew up to be a great prophet.

In the New Testament, it was the Temple leaders who had Christ crucified, yet after His resurrection and ascension, the disciples were "continually in the temple, praising and blessing God" (Luke 24:53).

When Jesus founded the church, He intended His followers to join it and remain faithful to it. Today, if you are among the more than fifty percent of the population of this country who have no active formal church affiliation, you may stand in bewilderment before the number whose membership is open to you. In selecting one you may well have a natural tendency to return to the church of your childhood, or you may feel you want to make a choice based on your more spiritually mature judgment. A church affiliation is not something to be entered into lightly, for if the church is to be of the greatest service to you, and even more important, if it is to give you the greatest possible opportunity to be of service to others, you must prayerfully select the one where you feel you can be of the most service to God.

A Church for Everyone

Some people find it easier to draw closer to God in magnificent buildings and with some form of ritual. Others find they can seek God only in stark simplicity. Some people find themselves more comfortable with formality, others feel more at home with informality. The important thing is not *how* we do it, but the sincerity and depth of purpose *with which* we do it, and we should each find and join the church in which as individuals we can best accomplish this.

Do not make the mistake of attaching yourself to a particular minister rather than to the body of the church itself. The ministry may change—it is healthy and stimulating that it should—but the tenets of the church remain the same, and it is to the church and its Christ that you owe allegiance. A stable church is built up when the members of the congregation recognize that it is their mutual love of Jesus Christ and the sincere desire to follow in His steps that hold them together.

The true Christian goes to church not only for what he gets out of it, but also for what he can put into it. He goes to add his prayers to those of others, he goes to add his voice to the other voices raised in praise of the Lord, he goes to add his strength in beseeching the Lord's blessing, he goes to add his weight of testimony to the possibility of salvation through the Lord Jesus Christ. He goes to join with others in the worship of God, in the contemplation of His boundless mercy and love. He also goes for the necessary companionship of fellow believers.

Christians who are not actively involved in the life of a local church remind me of what happens when a burning coal is removed from the fire. You've seen it happen. The coal gradually cools and its flame dies once it is removed from the bed of glowing coals.

In the far west, when the wolves attack a flock of sheep, the first thing they do is try to scatter them, and then they close in for the kill on one of the isolated sheep.

The Church Is a Channel

The church should be the means of channeling your funds for Christian work and the needs of fellow Christians. The Bible teaches tithing. A tithe is one tenth of your net income. That one tenth of your income belongs to the Lord. In addition to your tithe, you should give as the Lord has prospered you. Giving is a Christian grace that should be woven into the fabric of our daily lives until it becomes a part no longer distinguishable from the rest. Generosity should motivate us in all things.

Christ said, "It is more blessed to give than to receive" (Acts 20:35). He knew how giving warms the heart and satisfies the soul. He coveted for you that particular blessing. Selfishness is caused by fear—and a Christian should stand forth unafraid. Jesus stood always with hands that were open—not with hands that were clenched tight with selfishness and greed. As far as possible, one should give inconspicuously and quietly. Jesus also said that when we are giving, ". . . let not thy left hand know what thy right hand doeth" (Matthew 6:3).

Giving cannot be measured in dollars and cents, it cannot be measured in boxes of old clothes. Sometimes the greatest gift is the gift of friendship and neighborliness. A kind word, a friendly greeting, an evening spent with someone who is lonely can reap rich harvest for the kingdom of God. It is impossible for you to become a soul winner unless you are prepared to give something of yourself. Not only your money, but your time, your talents, your very self—everything is to be given to the service of Christ.

The giving of your offering which is above the tithe should not be limited by set rules or organized methods. It should be governed by the need that is brought to your attention according to the rules set down by Christ in Matthew 6:14. It might be a neighbor, the newsboy who brings the daily paper, or someone in far-off Africa or South America. Our giving is the expression of our love for God. We give back to Him in return for the great love He has bestowed on us, and in that way we spread His love abroad.

The Christian should also share in community responsibilities as time and money allow. The people to whom the money is given should know that you are giving it in the name of Christ. The letter accompanying the financial gift to the social or charitable organization should say something like, "As a Christian, believing the Lord would have me assist my community as I am able, I send this gift. God bless your efforts."

Be careful that you do not become guilty of the sin of robbing God. The Bible says, "Bring ye all the tithes into the storehouse, that there may be meat in mine house, and prove me now herewith, saith the Lord of hosts, if I will not open you the windows of heaven, and pour you out a blessing, that there shall not be room enough to receive it" (Malachi 3:10).

Dr. Louis Evans has said, "The gospel is free, but it costs money to provide the pails in which to carry the water of salvation."

The act of giving is just as much an act of worship as praying or singing. The United States Government now allows individuals to give up to fifty percent of adjusted gross income to charitable institutions and/or religious organizations. It is deductible from our income tax, and yet it is estimated that less than ten percent of the American people take advantage of this. Corporations are allowed to give up to ten percent, and yet only about fifteen percent of them are taking advantage of this provision of the government. Yet even if our government made no such allowance, ten percent still *belongs* to God.

The Church Spreads the Gospel

The churcn is for the spreading of the gospel. The church is commanded to "Go ye into all the world, and preach the gospel" and to baptize those who believe. The basic and primary mission of the church is to proclaim Christ to the lost. The need of the world today is sending forth its S.O.S., asking the church to come to its help. The world is being overwhelmed by social, moral, and economic problems. Its people are going down, swept under the waves of crime and shame. The world needs Christ. The mission of the church is to throw the lifeline to the perishing sinners everywhere.

Jesus said, "Ye shall receive power, after that the Holy Ghost is come upon you: and ye shall be witnesses unto me" (Acts 1:8). With the power of the Holy Spirit we can join hands with other Christians to win people to Christ. Sixty-five percent of the world has yet to hear the gospel of Jesus Christ. In this generation we have failed miserably to fulfill our mission to evangelize the world. According to the Wycliffe Bible translators, there are still more than three thousand languages and dialects into which the Bible has not been translated.

The early church had no Bibles, no seminaries, no printing presses, no literature, no educational institutions, no radio, no television, no automobiles, no airplanes; and yet within one generation the gospel had been spread to most of the known world. The secret of the spread of this gospel was the power of the Holy Spirit.

Today in the face of vastly improved methods of communication the power of the Holy Spirit is the same. We need not do things in our own strength and, as a result, fail.

Today the only feet that Christ has are our feet. The only hands, our hands. The only tongues, our tongues. We must use every talent, facility, and method possible to win men to Christ. This is the great mission of the church. Our methods may vary. We may use visitation evangelism, educational evangelism, preaching missions, industrial evangelism, cell evangelism, radio television evangelism, movie evangelism, or so-called mass evangelism.

I am aware today that in many parts of the world the church is outlawed, discredited, and at times virtually destroyed. Yet again and again it has been proven "The blood of the martyrs is the seed of the church." And God's church is a Bible-centered church, and it grows strong under persecution. "Where two or three are gathered, there am I in the midst of them" has become literally true in some parts of the world. In such places where believers in Christ live in abject poverty, they still tithe. And when one member suffers, the others come to that one's aid. Unable to preach openly, they look for opportunities to witness by life. So, for instance, when one is punished harshly for some unjust reason and bears it cheerfully, a curious observer will slip up to him and say, "I saw that. It was unfair. And yet you remain cheerful." And the Christian has the opportunity to share his faith in Christ.

So even where Christ's church suffers, she grows. What a challenge to us to do likewise!

17

Am I My Brother's Keeper?

And forgive us our debts, as we forgive our debtors.

Matthew 6:12

SINCE you have made your decision for Christ and have begun studying the Bible, you find yourself confronted with various social obligations and problems. You have made your peace with God. You are no longer at war and at enmity with God. Sin has been forgiven. You have new horizons for your thinking—new perspectives for your life. The whole world has changed. You now begin to see others through the eyes of Jesus. Old ideas and ideals have changed. Prejudices that you once held are beginning to slip away. Selfishness that was once characteristic of you in many areas of your life has now disappeared. Suddenly you understand what the little story means: Someone asked, "Am I my brother's keeper?" And the reply came, "No, I am my brother's *brother.*"

Many people have refused the Christian life because it has been presented to them in its negative rather than its positive aspect. They say that Christian conduct is against everything pleasant and profitable. They say Christians are like the woman who complained that everything worth doing in this life was either immoral, illegal, or fattening!

Contrary to worldly belief, being a true Christian does not mean the forfeiting of all real pleasure. Only sinful pleasure that has been forbidden by God is to be given up. The full acceptance of Christ and the determination to be guided by God's will draws you almost immediately to the source of the only true pleasure—which is fellowship with Christ. To you who have *not* been born again this may seem a far cry from pleasure, but those who have actually experienced daily fellowship with Christ know that it surpasses all worldly activities.

In his introduction to his anthology on George MacDonald, C. S. Lewis writes, "He seems to have been a . . . playful man, deeply appreciative of all the really beautiful and delicious things that money can buy and no less deeply content to do without them."

George MacDonald himself wrote: "I would, if I may, be ever greeted in my study in winter by a glowing hearth, and in the summer by a bowl of flowers. But if not, then let me think how nice they would have been and let me bury myself in my work. I do not think that contentment lies in despising what you have not got."

Even as the psalmist says, "They shall be abundantly satisfied with the fatness of thy house; and thou shalt make them drink of the river of thy pleasures" (Psalm 36:8). God has also said, "No good thing will he withhold from them that walk uprightly" (Psalm 84:11). Paul said that "[God has] given us richly all things to enjoy" (1 Timothy 6:17).

The fact that we have daily fellowship with Christ should enable us to live realistically. Christ's way of life does not require that a man renounce legitimate interests or ambitions. Though the Scriptures may teach that Christ may return at any time, the Scripture also exhorts us to carry on business as usual until He comes.

For example, there was nothing wrong about the eating, drinking, marrying, and giving in marriage in Noah's day except that the people had become totally preoccupied with these activities to the neglect of the spiritual dimension of life (Luke 17:27). Nor was there anything wrong about the buying, selling, planning, and building in Lot's day except that they were carried on by sinful methods (Luke 17:28). What seems to have been fundamentally wrong in the days of Noah and Lot was that men made these the sole interest of their lives. They thought of nothing but their personal pleasures, their personal property, and the material profits they were amassing. They became so absorbed in the things of this life that they had no time for God. This was displeasing to God, and He visited the offenders with judgment.

As someone has said, "The Bible was not written to encourage people to take an interest in the affairs of this life. It *assumes* that they already have more than their share of interest of that. The Bible aims to encourage man to see his worldly affairs in the light of the greater importance and value of spiritual things."

The Bible teaches that we are to perform our daily tasks and that we are to take pride in performing them well. We were put here on earth and given certain work to do, and those who claim to be Christians are taught not only to labor but to labor to the best of their ability.

The Bible speaks approvingly of Bezaleel as a worker in metals, stone, and wood. He was filled with the Holy

Spirit for *craftsmanship*: "And I have filled him with the spirit of God, in wisdom, and in understanding, and in knowledge, and in all manner of workmanship . . . to work in gold, and in silver, and in brass, and in cutting of stones, to set them, and in carving of timber, to work all manner of workmanship" (Exodus 31:3–5). Jacob and his sons were shepherds. Joseph was a prime minister. Daniel was a statesman. Both Joseph and Jesus were carpenters, and some of the disciples were fishermen. We are told of the Ethiopian eunuch who was treasurer under Candace; of Lydia, the seller of purple; of Paul, Priscilla, and Aquila who were tentmakers; and Luke, the beloved physician.

The Christian ideal certainly does not demand that a person renounce all interest in the affairs of this life; but rather that we seek God's guidance in performing our daily work to the best of our ability and that we keep both our work and our ambitions in subordination to the Lord at all times. Thus we find that Christ offers positive help in our daily living here on earth. He inspires us in our gifts, helps us in our work, and blesses us in our pleasure.

In one of his delightful essays, F. W. Boreham, quoting Isaiah, goes on to recount how the carpenter of Nazareth has encouraged the goldsmiths of the ages. The world's greatest writers have been inspired by Jesus of Nazareth, the greatest artists, musicians, and sculptors have also been illumined by Him.

He also helps in facing the social problems that confront us, and it is here that we may become confused. For it is in our daily tasks and in the way we face the social problems around us that the world will see Christ in us.

As my father-in-law, the late Dr. L. Nelson Bell, once wrote in the *Southern Presbyterian Journal*, "If you are in church on Sunday the people who see you there may *presume* that you are a Christian. But what about the people with whom you come in contact during the week on the street, in your office, in your store, and the multiple places where you make these inevitable daily contacts? Orthodox Christian profession has its place. Attendance at, and active participation in, the program and activities of the church are an inescapable part of Christian living. But we all know, the business of making a living, the responsibilities of a home, the daily routine all combine to test the reality of our Christian experience and faith. In these daily contacts what do others see? Can our week-day associates tell that we are Christians? Do casual acquaintances see anything in us to suggest that we are different from those who do not know Christ? Certainly one of the real tests of Christian character is to be found in the lives we live from day to day.

"The reality of our Christian profession is shown in many ways: the things we say, as well as the things we do not say; the things we do, as well as the things we do not do. For while Christianity is not primarily a matter of externals, nevertheless it does find expression in conversation, habits, recreation, emphasis, and ambitions to be noted in our daily life. Does our conversation honor Christ? Are our habits those of which He approves? Are our sources of recreation those in which His presence can be a part? Do we bow our heads in a word of thanks when eating in a public place? Can people tell from the emphasis we attach to material things whether we have set our affection on things above, or whether we are primarily attached to this world? Do people see in us an ambition for place and position out of accord with that of a Christian? We should ask ourselves these and many other questions, for in such things men judge whether we are Christians or not."

Some time after my father-in-law's death, my wife hired a man to help with some road work on our mountain property. One day, on the way to town, she stopped to speak to him. Suddenly he asked, "Is you Dr. Bell's daughter?" She admitted she was, whereupon the man exclaimed with deep appreciation, "Law! He was the awfullest Christian I ever knowed!"

What is our attitude toward those of other races? What is our attitude toward sex? What is our attitude toward the labor-management problems? What is our attitude toward the abortion issue, sexual deviation as an acceptable alternate lifestyle, drug and alcohol abuse and the problems inherent in them? All of these are very real and practical questions that must be answered, interpreted, and lived before our fellow men.

The guiding principle of our relation to the world about us should be, as Jesus said, "And as ye would that men should do to you, do ye also to them likewise" (Luke 6:31).

Many people have criticized the so-called "social gospel," but Jesus taught that we are to take the gospel to the world. Actually there is no such thing as a "social gospel." It is a misnomer. There is only one gospel. "If any man preach any other gospel to you, let him be accursed" (Galatians 1:9). At the same time, in 1 Timothy 5:8 we are told, "If any provide not for his own, and especially for those of his own house, he hath denied the faith, and is worse than an infidel." What a relief to the federal government if Christians made themselves responsible for the needs of their own!

My son, Franklin, is deeply involved in social work, heading up a Christian relief agency. In a recent interview he was quoted as saying that "proclaiming the gospel must always have priority." He urged evangelical relief and development agencies not to lose sight of the need to reach people for Christ. "The gospel—not development—is the Christian's mandate," he said.

The cup of cold water comes *after* and sometimes *before* rather than *instead of* the gospel. Christians, above all others, should be concerned with social problems and social injustices. Down through the centuries the church has contributed more than any other single agency in lifting social standards to new heights. Child labor has been outlawed. Slavery has been abolished in Britain, the U.S.A., and some other parts of the world. The status of women has been lifted to heights unparalleled in history, and many other reforms have taken place primarily as a result of the influence of the teachings of Jesus Christ. The Christian is to take his place in society with moral courage to stand up for that which is right, just, and honorable.

Be a Good Citizen

First: *the Christian should be a good citizen.* The Bible teaches that the Christian should be law-abiding. The Bible also teaches loyalty to country. A loyalty and love of country does not mean that we cannot criticize unjust laws. The Bible says that God is no respecter of persons. All should have equal opportunities. The government of God should be our model.

The Bible also teaches that we are to cooperate with the government. The apostle Paul exhorted Timothy to ". . . supplications, prayers, intercessions . . . for all men; for kings, and for all that are in authority . . ." (1Timothy 2:1, 2). Jesus was asked, "Is it lawful to give tribute?" Then He set the example forever by paying taxes. It takes money to run a government and to maintain law and order. The tax dodger is a civic parasite and an actual thief. No true Christian will be a tax dodger. Jesus said, we are to "render to Caesar the things that are Caesar's" (Mark 12:17). We ought to be more than taxpayers. To be simply law-abiding is not enough. We ought to seek and work for the good of our country. Sometimes we may be called upon to die for it. We are to be conscientious in our work as good citizens.

We should be generous and give to those who are in need and to those organizations who are faithfully and honestly ministering to those in need. We should enter into various activities such as the Red Cross, the Salvation Army, World Vision, Samaritan's Purse, the Tear Fund, and other good, constructive, and helping-hand organizations. At the same time, as responsible stewards we are to check our various organizations for trustworthiness and honesty and also to find if the relief given certain governments is given where designated.

Christians should be interested in orphanages, hospitals, asylums, prisons, and all social institutions. Jesus said, "Love the neighbor as thyself" (Matthew 22:39). Think of a country without any philanthropic enterprises whatever! No one would want to live in it.

I recall visiting a country in which there were both government and Christian homes for the elderly. In the Christian home we saw love in action, but in the government home the care was impersonal and perfunctory. The doctor who served both homes said that the people in the Christian home were not only happier but lived longer. We want to live where neighborly love prevails. We are to take our place in the community. Those in positions of responsibility are entitled to respect, support, and cooperation. "Let every soul be subject unto the higher powers. For there is no power but of God: the powers that be are ordained of God" (Romans 13:1).

Be Hospitable

Second: *Christians should be "given to hospitality"* (1 Timothy 3:2). The Bible teaches that our homes should be hospitable and that those who come in and out of our homes should sense the presence of Christ. The happiest Christian homes I know are those given to hospitality, where neighbors feel at home, where young people are welcome, where the elderly are respected, where children are loved. That which God has given to us should be shared with others. In doing so God will bless and prosper our homes.

A Proper View of Sex

Third: *we should have the Christian attitude toward sex.* Nowhere does the Bible teach that sex in itself is a sin, although many interpreters of the Bible would try to make it appear so. The Bible teaches that the *wrong use* of sex is sinful. For sex, the act by which all life on this earth is created, should be a wonderful, meaningful, and satisfying human experience.

Man, with his vile, self-destructive nature, however, has taken what was intended to be the most glorious and complete act of love between two people and made of it something low and cheap and filthy. Sex, stripped of total commitment, of mutual love, respect, and the sincere desire to give joy and fulfillment to the other person, becomes simply an animal act, about which the Bible warns us in no uncertain terms!

It is significant that the Bible is one of the world's most outspoken books on the subject of sex. It does not try to gloss over sex in either its right or wrong aspects. The sly, secret, embarrassed, "let's-pretend-it-doesn't-exist" attitude about sex is purely manmade.

In trying to overcome the mysterious "let's-not-talk-about-it" approach to sex, our present civilization has put far too much emphasis on the mechanics of it and far too little insistence on the spiritual atmosphere in which this overwhelming expression of human love must have its origin.

Our divorce courts bear tragic testimony to the inability of men and women to achieve this lasting and ever more beautiful relationship without a firm foundation of spiritual values.

Sex is a part of life that we cannot abolish, even if we would, for without it all life would cease. For sex, the act by which all life on this earth is perpetuated, should be a wonderful and meaningful human experience. Used rightly it can bring joy into the home. Used wrongly it can make it a hell. Use it wisely and it will become a wonderful servant. Use it wrongly and it will be a terrible taskmaster.

Christians feel a sense of outrage, a sense of violation, when they see sex emblazoned in newspaper headlines, exploited in advertisements, and used as a cheap lure outside theaters. They blush for their fellowmen that they can be so stupid, so gross, so indecent as to defile and distort the act by which all God-given life is bestowed.

A Christian View of Marriage

Fourth: it follows naturally that *those who take a Christian view of sex will take a Christian view of marriage.* Before you enter into a marriage, consider the real spiritual implications that make an earthly marriage binding in heaven. Little by little as we grow toward maturity, we learn to love, first our parents and our friends, and later the one person who is to share our life. We have already seen how difficult this process is, for it is passion and not love that comes naturally to the unregenerate sinner.

Many have the terrible misfortune of selecting their mates while they are still in the toils of the world, the flesh, and the devil, and while the man or woman they select is also still in the same condition. Is it any wonder then that so many marriages contracted by two spiritually ignorant souls, who most of the time are incapable of real and lasting love, end up in the divorce courts?

Marriage is a holy bond because it permits two people to help each other work out their spiritual destinies. God declared marriage to be good because He knew that man needed a helpmate and woman needed a protector. He desires that husbands and wives never lose sight of the original purpose of marriage. It is woman's role to love and help and reassure her husband in every way she can, and it is man's role to love and protect and provide for his wife and the children she bears, so that the home may be filled with God's peace and harmony. They are to submit to each other—to love each other.

Marriages entered into with a clear understanding of God's purpose and God's laws have no need for divorce courts. Marriages that fall short of this ideal (and it is appalling how many of them do) should first seek to learn what God expects of the husband and the wife and then pray for God's help and guidance in carrying out His commands.

A Christian Approach to Labor Management Problems

Fifth: *we are to take the Christian attitude in labor-management relationships.* The Bible says, "Whatever you do, put your whole heart and soul into it, as into work done for God, and not merely for men—knowing that your real reward, a heavenly one, will come from God, since you are actually employed by Christ, and not just by your earthly master. But the slacker and the thief will be judged by God Himself, Who naturally has no distinction to make between master and man. Remember, then, you employers, that your responsibility is to be fair and just towards those whom you employ, never forgetting that you yourselves have a Heavenly Employer" (Colossians 3:23–25, PHILLIPS).

If Christ could prevail in all labor-management relations we would rarely have strikes. There would not be these long drawn-out arguments in which both sides are unwilling to concede the rights of the other. Management would treat employees with generosity, and employees would be eager to put in a full day's work for their hire or what their contract calls for—for they would be working not only for wages. We can learn from the attitude of both employer and employees in Japan toward one another in this regard.

The Bible teaches that all honest work is honorable, and the Christian should be the most faithful, the most willing and efficient worker of all. He should stand out in a factory or shop as one who wants justice, but one who would not stoop to take unfair advantage.

By the same token, the Christian employer should treat his employees with a respect and generosity that will become an example for other employers. A man of real

Christian concepts cannot help being concerned about safety precautions, good working conditions, and the well-being of those in his employ. He will not only see his workers as "man power," but also as human beings.

Both management and labor should remember that the improved conditions and better understanding they now enjoy had their beginnings as the result of a great spiritual revival. The heritage of labor unions comes from the church and the mighty Wesleyan revivals of the eighteenth century. Social liberty for the working classes began when a Christian leader, Lord Shaftesbury, in the face of bitter family opposition, led a lifelong crusade for better working conditions, shorter hours, more pay, and fair treatment for the working man.

Had it not been for the spiritual revival of the eighteenth century, the gains that labor has made might not have been achieved, or might have been delayed until much later in our history. When some labor leaders talk of outlawing religion, disregarding God, the Bible, and the church, they should remember how much of what they have today is due to the power of the gospel of Christ.

Some labor leaders, as well as industrialists, have grown haughty, proud, rich, self-satisfied, and power-seeking. All of them should humble themselves before God, seek to recognize the needs of each other and their extreme dependence on each other, and above all, try to apply the Golden Rule in its most practical and realistic sense.

A Christian View of Other Races

Sixth: *the Christian looks through the eyes of Christ at the race question* and admits that the church has only partially solved this great human problem. We have let the sports world, the entertainment field, politics, the armed forces, education, and industry outstrip us. The church should have been the pace-setter. The church should voluntarily be doing what the federal courts in America are doing by pressure and compulsion. But in the final analysis the only real solution will be found at the foot of the cross where we come together in brotherly love. The closer the people of all races get to Christ and His cross, the closer they will get to one another.

The Bible says in Christ there is neither Jew nor Gentile, there is neither male nor female, neither Greek nor barbarian, neither rich nor poor. The Bible indicates that we are all one in Christ. The ground is level at the foot of the cross. When Christ opens our spiritual eyes we behold not color, nor class, nor condition, but simply human beings with the same longings, fears, needs, and aspirations as our own. We begin to see people through the Master's eyes. Become friends—invite them to your home.

A Christian View of Materialism

Seventh: *the Christian attitude should prevail in the matter of economics.* Jesus said a man's life does not consist in the abundance of the things which he possesses. Money is a good slave but a bad master. Property is to be used, enjoyed, shared, given, but not hoarded. Paul said that the *love* of money was the "root of all evil" (1 Timothy 6:10). Wealth has its place and its power, but it is not entitled to occupy the throne or swing the scepter. Covetousness puts money above manhood. It shackles its devotee and makes him its victim. It hardens the heart and deadens the noble impulses and destroys the vital qualities of life.

Beware of covetousness in every phase and form! All of us should keep ourselves from it through vigilance, prayer, self-control, and discipline. Life is not a matter of dollars and cents, houses and lands, earning capacity and financial achievement. Greed must not be allowed to make man the slave of wealth.

When Jesus was asked to settle an inheritance dispute between two brothers, He declined with a word of warning and with one of the magnificent parables with which He so frequently pointed out the earthly applications of heavenly messages. He told the story of the wealthy landowner who, in the midst of prosperity, envisioned even greater wealth and made long-range plans which would fill his life with all the physical comforts and personal glory that he held most dear. Apparently he was talented, economical, industrious, prudent, honest, and moral in all his dealings—but he was the victim of ambition and self-interest, as are so many others.

He measured his success in broad fields and full barns, and fed his soul on human vanities. His life was wrapped up in his riches and centered in himself, and he made his plans without thought of God or the uncertainty of life.

But God spoke the final word, and the plans that extended for years ahead were cut short by sudden death. The property he had amassed so painstakingly slipped through his cold fingers to be divided, scattered, and squandered by others, while he was left to stand before God with nothing to show for the life he had led on earth.

The Christian, above all others, should realize that we come into life with empty hands—and it is with empty hands that we leave it. Actually we can possess nothing—no property and no person—along the way. It is God who owns everything, and we are but stewards of His property during the brief time we are on earth. Everything that we see about us that we count as our possessions only comprises a loan from God, and it is when we lose sight of this all-pervading truth that we become greedy and covetous.

When we clutch an object or a person and say, "This thing is mine," when we look with envious eyes at what another person has and plan to "get it by fair means or foul," we are forgetting that no matter what we get, we can't take it with us when we go to make our final accounting before the seat of judgment.

This does not mean that earthly riches in themselves are a sin—the Bible does not say that. The Bible makes it clear that God expects us to do the best we can with the talents, the abilities, the situations with which life endows us. But there is a right way and a wrong way to acquire money and a right way and a wrong way to achieve power. Too many Christians have misunderstood this and taken a most sinful and damaging spiritual pride in being poverty-stricken, in standing by helplessly and saying, "God's will be done," as their children suffered and went untended. The apostle Paul said, "But if any provide not for his own, and especially for those of his own house, he hath denied the faith, and is worse than an infidel" (1 Timothy 5:8).

Jesus told one of His most revealing parables to illustrate this very point when He recited the story of the rich man who gave each of his servants a certain amount of money to invest while he was away in a far land. When he returned he found that some servants had made wise investments and his money was multiplied, and he praised them for their sound judgment and prudence; but the frightened, unimaginative servant who could think of nothing to do with the money but to hide it from thieves, he condemned.

Earn your money, as much as you can, according to God's laws, and spend it to carry out His commands. Give one tenth of it to the Lord, the firstfruits (Proverbs 3:9), tithe faithfully, for the Bible says that this is right and just. After you have given a tithe—gifts and offerings. Whenever you have any doubts about material values, get out your Bible and read what Jesus taught about money, read what He had to say about the earning of money and the use and distribution of wealth. Just ask yourself, "What would Jesus have done in this situation?" and be guided by that and that alone.

It was my privilege at one time to have among my close friends an extremely wealthy industrialist. One day as we were lunching together he calmly announced that the day before he had sold a certain product, his family clearing $13,000,000 on the deal. "But let me tell you what I discovered in the Scriptures this morning!" he exclaimed, changing the subject abruptly to his deepest interests. This man had his priorities in order.

A Christian View of Those Who Suffer

Eighth: *a Christian will be concerned about suffering humanity around him.* The great slum areas of your own country will become a burden to you. The poverty and suffering of thousands of people in your own neighborhood will become a concern to you. You will join with organizations and associations to help alleviate the suffering of humanity around you. Many people spend so much time in lofty enterprises that they make no contribution to suffering immediately at hand. Who is our neighbor? Whoever is closest to us. It could be a wife, a husband, a child, or those living next door. Our neighbor is that one closest to us—then in our city or country—then the world.

The Bible says the common people heard Jesus gladly. Wherever He went, He healed the sick. He comforted the sorrowful, He gave practical encouragement. Years ago, an Anglican bishop told me that he could think of no social organization in England which did not have its roots in some evangelical awakening (including the SPCA!). The Christian will be interested in helping build and develop hospitals, orphanages, old people's homes, and other charitable institutions that are trying to help the less fortunate. The Christian will be interested in doing his part to help share the great wealth of this country with the needy in other parts of the world. He will be a supporter of reputable national or international social organizations helping the unfortunate of the world. A word of caution here. When we're giving God's money to an organization it behooves us as good stewards to check out how this money is being spent. There are many responsible, worthwhile charitable ministries who deserve our support and prayers—there are others we should not support.

Nowhere in the Bible does it teach that we are to withdraw ourselves from society. Rather, it teaches quite the contrary. We are to join with others who are working to good purpose to help lift the unfortunate. God needs social workers, prison guards, policemen, doctors, hospital attendants, nurses, charity workers, and many other types of people who can help alleviate human suffering.

The motto of the Rotary Club is "Service above self." The motto of the Kiwanis Club is "We build." The motto of the

Lions Club is "Liberty, intelligence, our nation's safety." All of these ideas originated in Christianity. Lots of the pagan religions never had a service club. All of these organizations are really by-products of Christianity even when some of their members are not Christians. The perfume of Christ is in the fragrance of any and all social service.

Love for the Brethren

Ninth: *the Christian has a special obligation to fellow Christians.* Fellow Christians are in a special class. We are to have *supernatural love* for them. "We know that we have passed from death unto life, because we love the brethren. He that loveth not his brother abideth in death" (1 John 3:14).

We are to love our enemies. We are even to love those who persecute us and say "all manner of evil against us, falsely" (Matthew 5:11).

But the greatest of our human love is for those other believers. Jesus said, "This is my commandment, that ye love one another, as I have loved you" (John 15:12).

We are told to *serve* one another: "Brethren, through love be servants of one another."

Lord, help me to live from day to day
In such a self-forgetful way
That even when I kneel to pray
My prayers shall be for others.
Help me in all the work I do
Ever to be sincere and true,
And know that all I do for Thee
Must needs be done for others.
Others Lord; yes, others.

Let this my motto be.
Let me live for others
That I may live like Thee.
C. D. Heigs

The Bible says that our obligation to each other as Christians is such that we should be examples to each other. Paul said. "Be thou an example of the believers, in word, in conversation, in charity, in spirit, in faith, in purity" (1 Timothy 4:12). This is not a suggestion—it is a command! It is not a recommendation but an obligation. We are to be model Christians.

The Bible also says we are to *forgive* one another. "And be ye kind one to another, tenderhearted, forgiving one another, even as God for Christ's sake hath forgiven you" (Ephesians 4:32). Jesus said that if you will not forgive, neither will your Father which is in heaven forgive your sins. He also said, "When ye stand praying, forgive, if you have ought against any; that your Father also may forgive you" (Mark 11:25).

We are told as Christians *not to judge* one another, but rather decide never to put a stumbling block or hindrance in the way of a brother.

The Bible says that we are *to be subject* one to another; we are to clothe ourselves with humility toward each other. We are to be "in honor, preferring one another." We are to put others first, and ourselves last.

During the last six years of her life my mother-in-law was confined to a wheelchair as a result of a stroke. My father-in-law, Dr. L. Nelson Bell, who had been an extremely active athlete, physician, missionary, and writer (for the last year of his life he also served as moderator of the Southern Presybterian Church before its union), devoted himself totally and lovingly to her care. One day he said to my wife, "You know, these are the happiest days of our lives! Taking care of your mother is the greatest privilege of my life." And those of us who watched him care for her knew that he meant it.

As Christians we are to *bear one another's burdens*. There are burdens which every man must bear for himself for no one can do it for him, and if he neglects them they will not be borne. However, there are other burdens that our friends can help us bear, such as sorrow, misfortune, trials, loneliness, family cares, spiritual difficulties, a son or daughter on drugs or in prison—or a child who has disappeared. But we are not to worry about our burdens. We are to roll them on to God's shoulders, looking to Him for power to sustain and strengthen us. However, it is our duty to help our fellow man bear his own burden.

The Bible says as Christians also we are to *be generous* with each other. God says it is our duty as Christians to take care of widows and orphans and to help the poor within the Christian society. The Bible says: contribute to the needs of the saints . . . practice hospitality . . . lodge strangers . . . wash the saints' feet . . . relieve the afflicted . . . be not forgetful to entertain strangers. And Jesus said, "Inasmuch as ye have done it unto one of the least of these my brethren, ye have done it unto me. . . . It is more blessed to give than to receive." "God loveth a cheerful giver." All of these are our social obligations one to another as Christians.

Grace in Action

Lastly, Christians ought *to be gracious*, and this is one of the most important of Christian virtues—and one of the greatest.

The very power of our conviction sometimes inclines us toward feeling that we are right and that all other people are wrong. This is well and good when our convictions are based upon the "Thou shalts" and the "Thou shalt nots" of Scripture rather than our own ideas. The many different and frequently warring factions within the church emphasize the terrible human tendency to gather into select little groups, built upon profound convictions on trivial matters, each insisting that they and they alone have the right answer.

As the late Dr. Harry Ironside once said: "Beware lest we mistake our prejudices for our convictions."

To be sure we must deplore wickedness, evil, and wrongdoing, but our commendable intolerance of sin too often develops into a deplorable intolerance of sinners. Jesus hates sin but loves the sinner.

I was amused and shocked to hear a man of considerable religious background declare on television not long ago that "you didn't catch Jesus associating with questionable people or those whose basic ideas and attitudes were at variance with what Jesus knew to be honorable and right!"

Such a man should have known that Jesus wasn't afraid to associate with anyone! One of the things which the scribes and Pharisees criticized most bitterly was His willingness to help and talk to and exchange ideas with anyone, be they publicans, thieves, learned professors or prostitutes, rich or poor! Even His own followers decried some of the people with whom He was seen in public, but this did not lessen the compassion that Jesus felt for all the members of poor, blinded, struggling humanity.

Jesus had the most open and all-encompassing mind that this world has ever seen. His own inner conviction was so strong, so firm, so unswerving that He could afford to mingle with any group secure in the knowledge that He would not be contaminated. It is fear that makes us unwilling to listen to another's point of view, fear that our own ideas may be attacked. Jesus had no such fear, no such pettiness of viewpoint, no need to fence Himself off for His own protection. He knew the difference between graciousness and compromise, and we would do well to learn of Him. He set for us the most magnificent and glowing example of truth combined with mercy of all time and in departing said: "Go ye and do likewise" (Luke 10:37).

These are just a few of the scores of things that could be mentioned that are the social obligations of the Christian. He cannot withdraw himself as a hermit and live a solitary life. He is a member of society. Therefore, the teachings of Jesus deal frequently with our attitudes toward our fellow men.

Study the Bible, read it—and then live by it. Only then can you demonstrate to a confused world the transforming power of the indwelling Christ.

18

Hope for the Future

For the Lord himself shall descend from heaven with a shout, with the voice of the archangel, and with the trump of God: and the dead in Christ shall rise first: then we which are alive and remain shall be caught up together with them in the clouds, to meet the Lord in the air: and so shall we ever be with the Lord. Wherefore comfort one another with these words.

1 Thessalonians 4:16–18

SOME time ago the book review section of one of the great newspapers of America ran an article entitled, "The Literature of Doom." In it, they listed all the titles of books today that are dealing with the end of the world. Also a number of movies are coming out today that are called "Armageddon" movies. This concern about the last days has dramatically invaded the entertainment world. People are wondering whether there's going to be a world of tomorrow or not. There is concern about what is going to happen by the year 2000—or if we'll even reach that landmark year. Because of the tension in the world, the turmoil on almost every continent, some world leaders doubt we will survive beyond the year 2000—we seem to be getting worse and worse every day.

Some people ask the question, "When is Jesus Christ coming back?" He told us not to speculate about a certain day, but He did leave some signs that we'll discuss later. The coming again of Jesus Christ is mentioned in the Scripture more than 300 times in the New Testament alone. This shows that the Holy Spirit, who directed the writing of the Bible, puts tremendous stress on the fact that Christ is coming back to this earth again.

C. S. Lewis, the great Cambridge and Oxford professor, once said that there are three things which keep people from believing in the coming of Christ. First, he said Jesus didn't come when they expected Him to come in that first century. So people say, "Well, things are going on just as they have always gone, and He hasn't come. Why hasn't He come?" The second reason, he said, was the theory of evolution—the idea that we are making progress on our own, and we really don't need Christ. We're doing it ourselves! And the third reason, Lewis added, is that the coming of Christ cuts across our materialism and our good times—all the things that we like the most in this world. Even though he has been dead for some years now, Lewis saw our day with a perceptive eye.

Just a few days before president-elect John F. Kennedy was to be inaugurated, I was invited to join him and Senator George Smathers in Florida for a golf game and an evening visit at the Kennedy compound in Palm Beach. As we were driving back from the golf course, President Kennedy parked the car, turned to me, and asked, "Do you believe Jesus Christ is coming back to earth again?" I was dumbfounded at his question. For one thing, I never dreamed that Mr. Kennedy would ask a question like that, and for another, I wasn't even sure that he knew Jesus was supposed to come back! Having only been with him a few times prior to that incident I had no grasp of his religious knowledge. "Yes, sir, I do," I replied.

"All right," he said. "Explain it to me." So for several minutes I had the opportunity to talk to him about the second coming of Jesus Christ. I have often wondered why he asked that question, and I think part of the answer came a thousand days later when he was assassinated. Cardinal Cushing read the verses I've quoted at the beginning of this chapter at President Kennedy's funeral, and millions of people watched and heard the services around the world.

That statement in verse 17 especially stands out: we who are alive on that day will be caught up together with those who have gone before to meet the Lord in the air. That phrase, "caught up," is the translation of a Greek word which means to snatch away. The day is fast approaching when Jesus Christ will come back to "snatch away" His followers from all the graveyards of the world, and those of us who are alive and remain will join them in the great escape! That is the hope of the future for the Christian.

Because of the Promises of the Old Testament

Why is Christ going to come? There are five reasons why Christ has to come back to this earth. First, He must come back because of the promises of the Old Testament that have yet to be fulfilled. Scores of prophecies were fulfilled at His first coming. But some prophecies still remain to be fulfilled. For example, the Scripture says, "For unto us a child is born, unto us a son is given: and the government shall be upon his shoulder: and his name shall be called Wonderful, Counselor, The mighty God, The everlasting Father, The Prince of Peace. Of the increase of *his* government and peace there shall be no end, upon the throne of David and upon his Kingdom, to order it and to establish it with judgment and justice from henceforth even forever" (Isaiah 9:6, 7). Someone has said, "When our government is upon His shoulder, of its increase and of our peace there shall be no end."

That portion has not been fulfilled to completion. A child was born. A Son was given. But the government is not upon His shoulder. He did not bring world peace in that first coming, nor did He bring world justice at His first coming. But He's going to bring it the second time, because the Scripture teaches that all of these prophecies are going to be fulfilled. In Micah the prophet says, "He shall judge among many people, and rebuke strong nations afar off; and they shall beat their swords into plowshares, and their spears into pruning hooks: nation shall not lift up sword against nation, neither shall they learn war any more" (4:3). But consider the wars that are being fought right now. Look at the armament race that is escalating. Some day, however, men *are* going to make spears into pruning hooks; and some day, nation will not lift up sword against nation. Why? Because the Prince of Peace is coming back—He's going to be the world ruler.

Because of His Own Statements

Second, Christ has to return because of His own statements. He is absolute truth. Matthew 24 and 25 are entirely given over to statements about His coming again. For example, Matthew 24:27: "For as the lightning cometh out of the east, and shineth even unto the west; so shall also the coming of the Son of man be." The Bible again says in Matthew 25:31–32, "When the Son of man shall come in his glory, and all the holy angels with him, then shall he sit upon the throne of his glory: and before him shall be gathered all nations. . . ." This prophecy has yet to be fulfilled, but He said it and I believe it will be.

Jesus didn't lie to us. He said, "I go to prepare a place for you. And if I go and prepare a place for you, I will come again, and receive you unto myself; that where I am, there ye may be also" (John 14: 2, 3). He's going to come back in person. The Lord Jesus is coming back Himself! That's how much He loves us. The plan of salvation is not only to satisfy us in this world and give us a new life here, but He has a great plan for the future. For eternity!

The Bible says we are going to reign with Him. We're joint heirs with the Lord Jesus Christ, and we're going to spend eternity with Him! What is He doing now? He's preparing a home for us! It's been nearly two thousand years. What a home it must be! Eye cannot see nor ear hear, nor hath entered into the heart of man, what God has prepared for those who love Him!

Because of the Present Position of Satan

There is a third reason why Christ must come: the present position of Satan. The most powerful being in all the world today, outside of God Himself, is the devil. And the Bible says, strangely enough, that he has access to heaven itself—to the throne of God. The Bible says that he's the accuser of the brethren, night and day. He's called the anointed cherub—he's called the roaring lion—he's called the king of beasts. He's going about seeking whom he may devour. And at the temptation he showed Jesus all the kingdoms of the world, and he said in effect, "I will give you all of these if you will bow down and worship me" (Matthew 4:9). Jesus did not dispute him. Satan had the power to give Jesus the cosmos, the world system of evil. But, thank God, our Lord quoted Scripture, and that's one thing the devil can't stand! The Scripture defeats him every time.

In 2 Corinthians 4:4 he's also called "the god of this age." That means that he's the director of the false religions and philosophies of the world. The Bible says the whole cosmos (world) is under his control. What's going to transpire if something doesn't happen to Satan? Who's going to dispose of evil? Who's going to dispose of Satan? Humanity is helpless before him. Man is unable to chain him. The church cannot dethrone him. Legislation is impotent. The United Nations does not know how to handle him. They don't even understand that they're dealing with a spiritual power—an enormous power of evil in the world today.

Let's not forget one fact, however. There is One who is more powerful than Satan! This One defeated him two thousand years ago on the cross. The devil didn't want Jesus Christ to go to the cross, because he was afraid of what Christ would do on the cross. He knew that when Christ died on the cross, He was bearing the sins of the whole world. And God was saying to mankind from the cross, "I love you. I want to forgive you of all of your sins. I want you to be My child and one day to join Me in heaven." And if Jesus had come down from the cross, we couldn't be saved. We couldn't go to heaven. That's why the devil didn't want Him on the cross. That's why they taunted Him, "If thou be the Son of God, come down from the cross." Satan suffered his greatest defeat at the cross and in the resurrection of the Lord Jesus Christ.

But the devil is still loose, still in charge of the cosmos, the evil that is in the world. All the injustices, all the wars in the world, the devil is promoting—all the crime, all the wickedness, all the terrible things that are going on. In his supernatural power, he has a supernatural plan, even to try to dethrone God.

There's only one person in heaven or earth who can deal with the devil, and He's coming back to deal with him. He's going to throw Satan into the bottomless pit and ultimately into the lake of fire. Then there will be no devil anymore. We're going to be freed from this terrible pull of evil and the satanic power that has controlled the hearts of men for so many centuries. That's why Christ has to come. He's the only One who can do it. The world right now is looking for a deliverer, as I read in one of our magazines the other day: "Oh, that the world had a deliverer."

Because of the Present Chaos in the World

And then fourth, Jesus must return because of the present chaos in the world—a world everywhere racked with pain, suffering, hunger, war, murder, lust, greed, hate, fraud, and corruption. Every possible form of human government seems to be failing. Each new one seems to be unsuccessful in dealing with our problems. The world is becoming more helpless and more hopeless as we enter this terribly involved and complicated computerized technological age. The Scripture says, "Say to them that are of a fearful heart,

Be strong, fear not; behold your God will come with vengeance, even God with a recompence; he will come and save you" (Isaiah 35:4). Jesus Christ is going to save us from ourselves. There are many sociologists and scientists today who believe we have the capability to destroy ourselves. And we can. The human race has the power right now to destroy itself. But Christ is going to come. And just as man is ready to hurl those bombs at each other, He's going to come to set up His kingdom of righteousness and glory and peace and justice. What a world that's going to be!

Will you be ready?

Because of the Dead in Christ

The fifth reason Christ must come is the dead in Christ—those people who died believing in God and trusting Him. When I saw the film "The Holocaust," I thought of all those people who were murdered by Hitler—many of them true believers. Thousands of people have suffered injustice, and killings, and all that has gone on in history, as believers in Christ and wondered why they had to die. Many must have wondered why they had to suffer for their faith. Jesus is coming back, and there's going to be a great resurrection. Believers are going to be raised from the dead! And then those who are alive and remain shall be caught up in the air, and so shall we ever be with the Lord. When is that going to take place? We don't know the exact day, but I believe it's drawing near. It's certainly two thousand years nearer than when He made the prediction.

Jesus left some signs behind for us to watch for. He said, first of all, there will be intellectual and mental confusion and disturbances throughout the world: "Upon the earth distress of nations, with perplexity . . ." (Luke 21:25). That word "distress" means tossed from all sides. And that word "perplexity" means no way out. We as a human race are going to reach a point where there's no way out.

The Way Out

Jean-Paul Sartre wrote a book entitled *No Exit,* and he told us there is no exit from the human dilemma. No way out. I tell you, there is a way out. And that way is the Lord Jesus Christ.

Jesus also said there would be a collapse of morals just before He comes back. Jesus said, "Likewise, also as it was in the days of Lot; they did eat, they drank, they bought, they sold, they planted, they builded; but the same day that Lot went out of Sodom it rained fire and brimstone from heaven, and destroyed them all" (Luke 17:28, 29). Then He said, "Even thus shall it be in the day when the Son of man is revealed" (v. 30). "As it was in the days of Noah, so shall it be in the days of the coming of the Son of man" (Luke 17:26). In both instances, in Lot's day and in Noah's day, morals had collapsed, and moral fiber is collapsing all around us right now. The world is on an immoral binge such as it's never known in history. Jesus said just before He returns that will be the condition of the human race.

Third, Jesus also said there will be a falling away. That means that people who were believers will be falling away individually or collectively. And "many false prophets shall rise, and shall deceive many." Look at the false prophets we have today. Now "the Spirit speaketh expressly that in the latter times, some shall depart from the faith, giving heed to seducing spirits and doctrines of devils" (1 Timothy 4:1).

There will be a falling away from true faith. Many have a false idea of God and see a caricature of Christianity. They are not really true disciples of Jesus Christ. They have already unwittingly fallen away—maybe not intellectually. They may still believe, but they've fallen away in the way they live. Your life justifies what you believe. Jesus says, "By their fruits ye shall know them." And the devil is still coming around and saying, "Yea, hath God said?" trying to make us doubt His holy Word. A lot of false prophets are coming around today and saying, "This cannot be trusted." I tell you, the Bible was inspired by God from cover to cover. It is God's holy Word. And there are those who are telling us, "Jesus Christ was a mere man," that He was not God. He is a God-man. Equally God and equally man. Filled with love for us, so much that He died for us.

A fourth point: Jesus indicated there would be an increase in lawlessness. He said that as lawlessness spread, men's love for one another will grow cold (Matthew 24:12). Newspapers are filled with these accounts right now. Have you ever heard of such terrorism all over the world? Terrorist activities are increasing in almost every country. Because of modern technology, people don't know how to cope with it. Jesus said in Luke 21:9, "Ye shall hear of wars and commotions," and that word "commotions" carries with it the idea of rebellion against all authority. We're seeing that in many parts of the world. Jesus said that would be one of the signs. And then He said there will be peace conferences. Paul wrote, "For when they shall say Peace and safety; then sudden destruction cometh upon them" (1 Thessalonians 5:3). The prophet Isaiah wrote, "There is no peace, saith the Lord, unto the wicked" (48:22). Never before have we had so many people seeking peace. The United Nations goes into one emergency session after another. The Congresses and the Parliaments of the world are searching for peace. The leaders of the world—our secretary of state goes back and forth around the world seeking peace, trying to patch this little place here, and this place there. By the time he or she gets back to Washington, trouble has broken out somewhere else. Jesus said it would be like that: "Except those days be shortened, there should no flesh be saved: but for the elect's sake those days shall be shortened" (Matthew 24:22).

Then Jesus said something else: there would be a worldwide emphasis on evangelism and the proclamation of the gospel before He came back. "And this gospel of the kingdom shall be preached in all the world for a witness unto all nations; then shall the end come." For the first time in history, the gospel is now being heard all over the world. By radio, by television, by literature, by satellite in every part of the world. There's not a place that they could not hear the gospel. For the first time.

Now, what are we to do? How do we face this? First, we purify ourselves. The Scripture says, "Every man that hath this hope in him purifies himself." Do you have the hope of the coming again of the Lord Jesus Christ? Then you should live it—a pure life, a godly life, a surrendered life, a consecrated life. There's a sense in which we're sanctified when we receive Christ. There's a sense in which we grow in the grace and knowledge of Christ in progressive sanctification. But one day we shall see Jesus face to face, and total sanctification is when we're perfect, as He is perfect. We shall see Him as He is.

Second, we are to wait with patience. I know sometimes we get a little anxious and wonder if Jesus is really going to come back. The Scripture says, "For you have need of patience, for yet a little while, and he that shall come will come, and will not tarry" (Hebrews 10:37). He has appointed a day. God knows the day. It's all set. He will be back right on time—He won't be an hour late or an hour early.

The third thing we're to do is to watch. That word "watch" means that we are to desire His coming. We are to be constantly thinking about His coming. At the beginning of this chapter I quoted the verse, "Looking for that blessed hope and glorious appearing."

The fourth thing is that we're to work. People say, "Well, Christ is coming back—let's quit all these activities that we're involved in." No! He may not come for a hundred years, or a thousand years. He may not come in our lifetime. Let's do our best to help reach our fellow man for Christ. His return should be our incentive toward work.

The last point: we're to be prepared. Are you prepared? "Be ye therefore ready also: for the Son of man cometh at an hour when ye think not" (Luke 12:40). The Scripture says, "By faith Noah being warned of God of things not seen as yet, moved with fear, prepared an ark to the saving of his house." That word "fear" means terrified. Yes! Some people are drawn into the kingdom of God by love and some come into it in terror. We have a right to be terrified. Because for those who know not Jesus Christ as their Lord and Savior, it means judgment, it means hell. We must come to Christ while we can.

19

Peace at Last

And God shall wipe all tears from
their eyes; and there shall be no more death,
neither sorrow, nor crying, neither shall
there be any more pain. . . .
Revelation 21:4

IN THIS BOOK we have been looking at what it means to be at peace with God. We now know what it means to be a Christian. We know the price that was paid to get this illusive thing called peace and happiness. I know men who would write a check for a million dollars if they could find peace. Millions are searching for it. Every time they get close to finding the peace found only in Christ, Satan steers them away. He blinds them. He throws up a smoke screen. He bluffs them. And they miss it! But we Christians have found it! It is ours now forever. We have found the secret of life.

The word "peace" has been used often in the last forty or fifty years. We talk about peace, and we have many peace conferences; yet at the moment it seems that the world is heading toward anything but peace.

"The way of peace have they not known," the apostle Paul says concerning the human race (Romans 3:17). As we look around, we find that there is little personal, domestic, social, economic, or political peace anywhere. Why? Because we all have the seeds of suspicion and violence, of hatred and destruction within us.

Jesus said, "Blessed are the peacemakers" (Matthew 5:9). We are to try for peace. This does not mean pacifism. We are to work for peace. But Jesus also predicted: "Ye shall hear of wars and rumors of wars: see that ye be not troubled: for all these things must come to pass, but the end is not yet. For nation shall rise against nation, and kingdom against kingdom" (Matthew 24:6–7).

Peace can be experienced only when we have received divine pardon—when we have been reconciled to God and when we have harmony within, with our fellow man and especially with God. "There is no peace, saith my God, to the wicked" (Isaiah 57:21). But through the blood of the cross, Christ has made peace with God for us and is Himself our peace. If by faith we accept Him, we are justified by God and can realize the inner serenity that can come to man through no other means. When Christ enters our hearts, we are freed of that haunting sense of sin. Cleansed of all feeling of contamination and unfitness, we can lift up our heads secure in the knowledge that we can look with confidence into the face of our fellow men. "When a man's ways please the Lord he maketh even his enemies to be at peace with him" (Proverbs 16:7). Even more important, we know that we can stand before God in the hour of our death with this same feeling of peace and security.

In the Bible Jesus told us there is going to be war until the end of the age. He knew that human nature is not going to change without a spiritual new birth. He knew that the vast majority of the human race were never going to be converted to Him. The vast majority of the people of the world today are not "born again." So we always have the potential that violence will break out in a home, in a community, in the world.

There are three kinds of peace described in the Bible.

Peace with God

First, peace *with* God. "Therefore being justified by faith, we have peace with God through our Lord Jesus Christ" (Romans 5:1). "Having made peace through the blood of his cross . . ." (Colossians 1:20). There is a peace that you can have immediately—peace with God.

The greatest warfare going on in the world today is between mankind and God. People may not realize that they're at war with God. But if they don't know Jesus Christ as Savior and if they haven't surrendered to Him as Lord, God considers them to be at war with Him. That chasm has been caused by sin. The Bible says that all have "sinned and come short of the glory of God" (Romans 3:23). "Oh," people say, "I have joined the church. I have been baptized." But has Jesus come to live in their hearts? Not only as Savior, but as Lord?

It would be the greatest tragedy if I didn't tell you that unless you repent of your sins and receive Christ as your Savior, you are going to be lost.

"For God so loved the world, that he gave his only begotten Son, that whosoever [that "whosoever" is you] believeth in him should not perish, but have everlasting life" (John 3:16). It's not just head-belief. It's heart-belief too. It's total trust, total commitment. We bring everything to the cross where the Lord Jesus Christ died for our sins. He made peace with God by His death on the cross. If we turn our backs on Him and don't commit our lives to Him, we will have no hope in the future.

For one to have peace with God, it cost the blood of His Son. "With the precious blood of Christ, as of a lamb without blemish and without spot," said Peter (1 Peter 1:19). If I were the only person in all the world, Jesus would have died for me, because He loves me. And He loves you! His love is pouring out from the cross.

"Meet Me in Heaven"

I read a biography of Queen Victoria, and I learned that the queen would sometimes go to the slums of London. She went into one home to have tea with an older lady, and when the queen rose to leave, she asked, "Is there anything I can do for you?" And the woman said, "Yes, ma'am, Your Majesty, you can meet me in heaven." The queen turned to her and said softly, "Yes. I'll be there, but only because of the blood that was shed on the cross for you and for me." Queen Victoria, in her day the most powerful woman in the world, had to depend on the blood of Christ for her salvation. And so do we. The Bible says that God is the Author of peace (1 Corinthians 14:33). God provided salvation through the cross. He made peace by the shedding of His blood. The war that exists between you and God can be over quickly, and the peace treaty is signed in the blood of His Son Jesus Christ.

Are you at peace with God? Or do the sins of your heart separate you from God?

The Peace of God

The second peace spoken of in the Bible is the peace *of* God. Everyone who knows the Lord Jesus Christ can go through any problem, and face death, and still have the peace of God in his heart. When your spouse dies, or your children get sick, or you lose your job, you can have a peace that you don't understand. You may have tears at a graveside, but you can have an abiding peace, a quietness.

A psychiatrist was quoted in the newspaper as saying that he could not improve upon the apostle Paul's prescription for human worry. Paul said, "Be [anxious] for nothing; but in every thing by prayer and supplication with thanksgiving let your requests be made known to God. And the peace of God, which passeth all understanding, shall keep your hearts and minds through Christ Jesus" (Philippians 4:6–7). Be anxious for nothing. How many times do you and I fret and turn, looking for a little peace? God's peace can be in our hearts—right now.

Colossians 3:15 says, "Let the peace of God rule in your hearts." Some of you believe that you know Jesus Christ as your Savior, but you haven't really made Him your Lord. You're missing the peace of God in your struggles and turmoils and trials and pressures of life. Is the peace of God in your heart?

We are all familiar with the transformation that took place in Saul on the road to Damascus, when Christ entered his heart and changed him from one of His most destructive enemies to one of His mightiest advocates. Many equally dramatic changes in human personalities are taking place today, and they are being brought about by the self-same means that transformed Saul into Paul—birth again through Jesus Christ!

There is no human philosophy that can achieve such changes or provide such strength. This mighty strength stands ready to be available at your beck and call at all times. God said, "Fear thou not; for I am with thee: be not dismayed; for I am thy God: I will strengthen thee; yea, I will help thee; yea, I will uphold thee with the right hand of my righteousness" (Isaiah 41:10).

Whatever the circumstances, whatever the call, whatever the duty, whatever the price, whatever the sacrifice—His strength will be your strength in your hour of need.

There are physical benefits that accrue from Christian living. Sin and the sense of inner unworthiness impair physical and mental well-being. The sense of physical impurity and physical immorality, the sense of hatred directed toward our fellow men, the awareness of our own inadequacy and frustration and our inability to achieve the goals to which we aspire—these are the real reasons for physical and mental illness. The sense of guilt and sin that natural man carries within himself renders him unfit for the performance of his duties, renders him sick in both mind and body. It was no accident that Jesus combined healing with His preaching and teaching when He was on earth. There is a very real relationship between the life of the spirit and the health of the body and mind.

Peace with God and the peace of God in a man's heart and the joy of fellowship with Christ have in themselves a beneficial effect upon the body and mind and will lead to the development and preservation of physical and mental power. Thus, Christ promotes the best interest of the body and mind as well as of the spirit, in addition to inward peace, the development of spiritual life, the joy and fellowship with Christ, and the new strength that comes with being born again.

There are certain special privileges that only the true Christian can enjoy. There is, for example, the privilege of *having divine wisdom and guidance continually.* The Bible says, "If any of you lack wisdom, let him ask of God, that giveth to all men liberally, and upbraideth not; and it shall be given him" (James 1:5).

Also the Christian has a sense of *true optimism,* the assurance that according to divine revelation everything will turn out well in the end.

The Christian also has a *world view.* This world view sets forth God's purpose and the end toward which all are proceeding. It assures us that in spite of men's war upon each other and in spite of the destructive forces of nature which seem to hold us in their grip, God is still on the throne and in command of everything. Satan himself is held back by God's power and given an opportunity to exercise his evil influence only as God sees fit and only as long as God sees fit to let him do it. The Scriptures teach us that God has a definite plan for each period of history, for every nation, and for every individual. The Scripture discloses God's plan for the return of Christ when His kingdom shall be established, as we have already seen. Thus, for the Christian, life has a plan and an assurance that God will ultimately triumph over all unrighteousness.

In summing up the superiority of the Christian life over all other ways of living we cannot overlook the advantage that the Christian will have for all eternity. Job said, "If a man die, shall he live again?" (14:14). He answered his own question when he said, "For I know that my Redeemer liveth and that he will stand at the latter day upon the earth" (Job 19:25).

What a prospect! What a future! What a hope! What a life! I would not change places with the wealthiest and most influential person in the world. I would rather be a child of the King, a joint-heir with Christ, a member of the Royal Family of heaven!

I know where I've come from, I know why I'm here, I know where I'm going—and I have peace in my heart. His peace floods my heart and overwhelms my soul!

The storm was raging. The sea was beating against the rocks in huge, dashing waves. The lightning was flashing, the thunder was roaring, the wind was blowing; but the little bird was asleep in the crevice of the rock, its head serenely under its wing, sound asleep. That is peace: to be able to rest serenely in the storm!

In Christ we are relaxed and at peace in the midst of the confusions, bewilderments, and perplexities of this life. The storm rages, but our hearts are at rest. We have found peace—at last!

Future Peace

The third peace the Scriptures mention is *future* peace. The Bible promises that there will be a time when the whole world is going to have peace. It seems that the world is heading toward Armageddon. In Revelation 6:4 John the beloved apostle says there's a red horse, "and power was given to him that sat thereon to take peace from the earth." We're not going to have peace—permanent peace—until the Prince of Peace comes.

And He is coming. One of these days the sky is going to break open and the Lord Jesus Christ will come back. He will set up His reign upon this planet, and we're going to have peace and social justice. What a wonderful time that's going to be!

Isaiah predicted, "The government shall be upon his shoulder: and his name shall be called Wonderful, Counselor, The mighty God, The everlasting Father, The Prince of Peace. Of the increase of his government and peace there shall be no end" (Isaiah 9:6–7). Think of it: no fighting, no war, no hatred, no violence. It will all be peace.

To Be with Christ

Do you know Christ? Are you sure He's in your heart? Perhaps you have been thinking, "I want to be sure I have peace with God. I want to be sure that I'm ready for death. I want my sins forgiven. I want my guilt removed. I want to be with Christ when He comes and sets up His Kingdom."

It's all yours, and it's free. You don't have to work for it. "For by grace are ye saved through faith; and that not of yourselves: it is the gift of God: not of works" (Ephesians 2:8–9).

Give your heart and life to Christ now. Do not put it off.

20

The Day After

It is appointed unto men once to die,
but after this the judgment.
Hebrews 9:27

A FEW years ago, one of the television networks aired a program called "The Day After." At the end, it was as if the entire earth was a cemetery littered with corpses. For millions, this picture was a disturbing and traumatic experience.

If imagining such a possible nuclear winter experience would cause millions to think of their future, how much more so should the fact that however the end may come for them, the real "day after" for those who reject Christ is not this grim oblivion but *even worse* judgment and eternal hell, which would make the T.V. portrayal seem like a picnic in comparison!

But your future does not hinge on the world situation, however grim it might become. It depends on what happened 2,000 years ago at the cross and your acceptance or rejection of the Prince of Peace.

In updating this book, it has been our prayer that you will not delay finding the end of your Quest a moment longer. The time is far shorter than it was when this manuscript was originally written. Few of us know for certain when death will come for us. Make your *Peace with God* today.

O God, I am a sinner; I am sorry for my sin; I am willing to turn from my sin. I receive Christ as Savior; I confess Him as Lord; I want to follow Him and serve Him and others in the fellowship of His church. In Christ's Name, Amen.